Strategic Climate Change Communications

Effective Approaches to Fighting Climate Denial

Edited by
Jasper Fessmann

Climate Change and Society

 VERNON PRESS

www.vernonpress.com

In the Americas:
Vernon Press
1000 N West Street,
Suite 1200, Wilmington,
Delaware 19801
United States

In the rest of the world:
Vernon Press
C/Sancti Espiritu 17,
Malaga, 29006
Spain

Climate Change and Society

Library of Congress Control Number: 2019936183

ISBN: 978-1-62273-630-0

Cover design by Vernon Press using elements by:

Justin Brice Guariglia; Francesco Ungaro from Pexels; TheDigitalArtist from Pixabay.

"The road we have long been traveling is deceptively easy, a smooth superhighway on which we progress with great speed but at its end lies disaster. The other fork of the road – 'the one less traveled by' – offers our last, our only chance to reach a destination that assures the preservation of our earth."

Rachel Carson, Silent Spring, 1962.

Table of contents

Acknowledgements

First and foremost, I would like to thank the contributing authors. Each of them graciously gave their chapter to this book because they feel passionate about the dangers of global warming and wanted to offer practical solutions.

This book was written by activists and scholars to help activist communicators and environmental journalists to become more strategic and thus more effective. It is intended to help the environmental journalists to better resist manipulation by professional climate denial communicators using the science of public relations (PR) to promote vested interests. Although these "black sheep" of PR only represent a small subset of PR professionals (who mostly strive hard to work ethically) their work had an enormous impact on climate change – stymying meaningful progress on the issue for over three decades through highly effective strategic communications. A central tenet of the book is that these same PR skills and strategies used by deniers are some of the best weapons to fight the negative narratives generated by the climate change deniers.

The authors (alphabetical order):

- **Cynthia Barnett** - Environmental journalist and author specializing in water and climate, and Environmental Journalist in Residence at the University of Florida's College of Journalism and Communications. Besides many science and environmental articles, she has written three books: *Mirage: Florida and the Vanishing Water of the Eastern U.S.; Blue Revolution: Unmaking America's Water Crisis* and *Rain: A Natural and Cultural History.*

- **John Cook, PhD** - Research Assistant Professor at the Center for Climate Change Communication at George Mason University and founder of the Skeptical Science website. He is the co-author of three books: *Climate Change: Examining the Facts; Climate Change Science: A Modern Synthesis* and *Climate Change Denial: Heads in the Sand.*

- **Nicole Dahmen, PhD** - Associate Professor at the University of Oregon School of Journalism and Communications. Her research focuses on ethical and technological issues in visual communication, with an emphasis on photojournalism in the

Digital Age. She also has a special interest in contextual reporting, specifically solutions journalism and restorative narrative.

- **Jasper Fessmann, PhD** - Visiting Assistant Professor of Strategic Communications at the Reed College of Media at West Virginia University. He has dedicated his life and research to public interest communications (PIC) with a special focus on climate change communications. He is also a 15 PR agency veteran from Germany.

- **Nancy LaPlaca, J.D.** - Consultant at LaPlaca and Associates; Senior Fellow on Regulatory Issues at the Energy & Policy Institute – a watchdog organization exposing the attacks on renewable energy and countering misinformation by fossil fuel interests.

- **David L. Morris II, PhD** - Assistant Professor of Communication at the University of South Carolina Aiken. His research focus is at the intersection of visual communication, science communication, and technology. With this focus, he explores visuals of climate change messaging and their relationship to emotion, demographics, and psychographics.

- **Ishana Ratan** - PhD student in the Department of Political Science, University of California, Berkeley. Her research focused on international relations and statistical methodology. Prior, she worked as an international trade paralegal in Washington DC.

- **Anthony Karefa Rogers-Wright** - Deputy Director at RegeNErate Nebraska. He has presented the case for climate justice, environmental justice, and climate change action at universities nation- and worldwide and has written on the subjects for various publications. His first book *IntersectionALL: Missed Opportunities and New Possibilities for the Climate Community* is set for release in 2019.

- **Kim Sheehan, PhD** - Professor at the University of Oregon School of Journalism and Communications. A prolific scholarly author, she has written or edited 11 books in addition to 34 peer-reviewed articles and book chapters. She also has 12 years of practical experience in advertising and marketing.

I would like to thank my wife Anja Fessmann and the team at Vernon Press for their support. I would also like to warmly thank our peer-reviewers for their contributions:

- **Linda Hon, PhD** - University of Florida

- **Ah Ram Lee, PhD** - University of Massachusetts Amherst

- **Barbara Myslik** - University of Florida

- **Toluwani C. Oloke, PhD** - State University of New York at Fredonia

- **Ronen Shay, PhD** - St. John Fisher College

- **Xiaochen "Angela" Zhang, PhD** - Kansas State University

Furthermore, I would like to express my appreciation for environmental artist Justin Brice Guariglia for his overall work of visualizing climate change and his permission to use in the cover picture his arm, which has on it an evolving tattoo that tracks NASA's global temperature anomalies 5-year mean index.

Finally, I would like to thank the scholar and journalist who inspired this book:

- **Neela Banerjee** - Pulitzer Finalist and Senior Correspondent at InsideClimate News.

- **Cynthia Barnett** - Environmental Journalist in Residence at the University of Florida's College of Journalism and Communications.

- **Naomi Oreskes, PhD** - Professor of the History of Science and Affiliated Professor of Earth and Planetary Sciences at Harvard University.

Thank you all!

Jasper Fessmann
Editor

Foreword:
Climate Truths in a Post-Truth World

Cynthia Barnett

As I write in the fall of 2018, Hurricane Florence has swept out of North Carolina, but the heartbreak of flooding from coastal surge and the 10 trillion gallons of rain the storm dumped on America's Piedmont will surely last a generation. More than 50 people have died, including in drownings; numerous bridges and roads are washed away; hog lagoons and coal-ash pits have spilled dangerous waste into inland rivers; those rivers have breached countless rural towns; cotton, corn and other crops are sunk in billion-dollar farm losses; and more than 700,000 residential and commercial properties lay damaged in North Carolina, South Carolina and Virginia (Centopani, 2018).

All from a Category 1 hurricane. As the floodwaters recede, a number of scientific and data analyses point to a number of ways that climate change made the impacts of Florence much worse: Computer models show the catastrophic rains were 50 percent worse due to warmer temperatures in the atmosphere and seas. One in five homes swamped by the storm surge would have stayed dry if not for climate-driven sea-level rise, another study found (Crimmins et al., 2016; Reed, Stansfield, Wehner, & Zarzycki, 2018).

For the people of the Piedmont, the misery in the noxious floodwaters has also been made worse by climate denial: For six years in North Carolina, it has been illegal for policymakers to use up-to-date computer models to plan for rising seas in coastal development. Real estate, homebuilders and other business interests pushed the 2012 law to ensure Tar Heel building permits would not be slowed by a state commission report that showed sea-levels could rise as much as 39 inches by 2100. The report was meant to "take a hard look at this long-term problem," and help North Carolina adapt to a warming world, one of its authors, East Carolina University professor Stanley Riggs, told the *New York Times*. But, "we blew it" (Schwartz & Fausset, 2018, par 4). The 2012 law and subsequent action – and nonaction – by North Carolina's state government weakened coastal development policies and environmental regulations at just the time citizens needed more protection from rising seas, extreme rains other risks heightened by climate change.

North Carolina's legislated denial is but a portrait in miniature of the large-scale white-washing of climate science underway in the United States. The white-washing far predates U.S. President Donald Trump, though in him it has found one of its most-ardent fabulists. The president has called climate change a "hoax" and has directed rollback of dozens of environmental and climate regulations in the very same years Americans are beginning to endure the consequences of warming, from worsening storms and wildfires to increasing incidents of harmful algal blooms to spikes in childhood asthma and more heat-related deaths.

Indeed, widespread white-washing of science is not new; denial dates at least to Galileo's conviction on heresy for arguing the Earth could not be center of the Universe. But one hundred years ago, a new industry called public relations would prove so skilled at it that scientific facts would fall as precipitously as in Galileo's time. Science has never recovered. And neither has truth.

Ivy Ledbetter Lee – "a paid liar," Carl Sandburg called him – was a founder of the emerging field, which he alternately called "publicity" and "propaganda." As he explained the latter term: "The effort to propagate ideas." In 1914, Lee set out to propagate a better image for J.D. Rockefeller Jr., who had been vilified in the press, particularly by muckraker Ida Tarbell in her *McClure's* magazine series on "The History of Standard Oil." Lee produced a series of credible bulletins – later collected into a book called *Facts* – that succeeded in turning around the Rockefeller narrative in newspapers and the public consciousness (Lepore, 2018).

In reality, though, "Lee argued that facts don't exist, or at least, they can't be reported," writes the Harvard historian Jill Lepore in *These Truths: A History of the United States* (2018). "The effort to state an absolute fact is simply an attempt to achieve what is humanly impossible," Lee pronounced in a speech to journalism teachers in the 1920s. "All I can do is to give you my interpretation of the facts."

Rather, paying customers' interpretations of the facts. Like today, even weather disasters, themselves, were up for interpretation. When the deadliest hurricane in Florida's history roared through South Florida in September 1928, the Red Cross reached out nationally for donations to help victims, which included about 18,000 homeless families. The organization tapped President Calvin Coolidge to appeal to Americans to help "the great suffering which now needs relief and will need relief for days to come." Florida real estate and railroad interests were horrified the news would slow the 1920s land boom, which had already begun to collapse. They took out full-page ads in newspapers across the United States denying the scope of the disaster. Titled "The Truth About Storm Damage In Florida," one ad, like Lee's book of *Facts*, established credibility in the form of personal testimony: "Florida – the world's winter playground – with its unmatched climate, its fertile soil which has no superior, the length of the seasons, its freedom from the rigors of winters, all will continue to prosper and grow, and the area affected by this storm will take on a new aspect, *profiting by the experience gained.*" The at least 2,500 dead, and many more thousands homeless, would not appear to be profiting. The Red Cross estimated the propaganda cut into its budget for helping storm victims by at least a third (Drye, 2018).

That crass distortion could not help Florida's thinning real estate bubble, any more than the next crass PR campaign – on behalf of the tobacco industry – could save one of the estimated 7 million people globally who die each year from cigarette smoking. In the 1930s, the presidents of America's four largest tobacco companies turned to public relations to challenge the emerging science that cigarettes could kill. They hired one of the nation's top PR firms, Hill and Knowlton. The firm's founder and CEO, John Hill, set about "to deceive the American public about the health effects of smoking," as the U.S. Department of Justice later put it. Spinning existing science and funding new research to raise questions in smokers' minds, writes the Harvard historian of science Naomi Oreskes in *Merchants of Doubt* (Oreskes, & Conway 2011), the campaign succeeded by highlighting doubt. "Scientific doubts must remain," John Hill declared.

His company spent the next half-century making sure of it.

Many of the same scientists hired in the tobacco campaign, and the scientific-sounding organizations that it spawned, were later active in casting doubt on the scientific evidence for numerous other environmental and public health hazards. These included acid rain, the ozone hole, the industrial chemicals exposed by Rachel Carson in *Silent Spring*, and now, perhaps most devastatingly, the science of climate change (Michaels, 2008).

From casting the careful researcher Carson as "hysterical" half a century ago to claiming the rise in earth's temperatures is "natural" today, manipulative publicity has caused the planet untold harm. Now, the strengthening field of public interest communications aims to deploy strategy on behalf of a better world as deftly – or more so – as those who would plant denial in the science of smoking and carbon emissions.

Those communicating professionally on behalf of a better world have always been there, too; Carson was one of them. Her monumental conclusions about the impacts of synthetic chemicals on the web of life were first informed by her work as a writer for the U.S. Bureau of Fisheries (now the U.S. Fish and Wildlife Service). During sixteen years with the Service, she wrote numerous pamphlets, radio scripts and bulletins on conservation, including a popular series called Conservation in Action ("Rachel Carson: A Conservation Legacy", n.d.).

The problem, explains Jasper Fessmann in his history of public interest communications (2018a), is that development of sophisticated communications strategy for private vested interests has not (yet) been matched in the public sphere. And journalism, rather than becoming savvier to such strategy, has become ever more vulnerable amid financial strain and deep layoffs. There are approximately six public relations professionals for every journalist (Schneider, 2018), a gap that has widened as newsroom employment in the United States dropped 23 percent between 2008 and 2017. Nearly two hundred studies of the relationship between the fields reveal that between half and 75 percent of media content either comes directly from or is significantly influenced by public relations, finds the mass communications scholar Jim Macnamara (2016).

The complex threat of climate change churns this mediascape into something of a perfect storm. It is a test for public-interest communicators and journalists alike; no less than a test for the viability of truth in a post-truth world. In the chapters that follow, Fessmann and other public interest communicators well-describe the amoral, billion-dollar strategy underway to keep climate denial in the American mind, and what can be done to overcome it. Even a hint of doubt is all it takes for industry to make its case against regulations, now being repealed at breakneck speed. The Trump Administration has scrapped America's Clean Power Plan to reduce the emissions causing climate change; repealed methane rules; nullified federal rules on coal power plants; weakened fuel economy rules and car emissions standards; cut numerous climate- and renewable-energy research programs; loosened regulations on toxic air pollution; and expelled the words "climate change" from websites and emergency-management plans in one of the most expensive years of natural disasters in modern U.S. history.

Such actions are dangerous enough, Fessmann says, that we should consider ourselves at war with denial (2018b); that, after all, is how some polluting industry sees its battle against regulation. As traditional PR uses strategy, tactics and objectives that originated in strategic military science, he argues, a better understanding of such thinking is crucial for practitioners of public-interest communications, for scientists and for the journalists who cover climate change and its impacts.

At the very least, Fessmann argues, journalists and scientists must be sophisticated in their ability to recognize PR strategy, in order to bring light to the truths that it is trying to obscure. Specialization in Environmental Journalism is an important part of that effort. The better journalists' training and expertise, the better equipped they are to report on peer-reviewed science; avoid the false balance offered up by manipulative publicists; recognize greenwashing and front think-tanks; and treat press releases as tips rather than storylines.

The truth does, ultimately, come out. Seven million people die of lung cancer in a year's time. The rising floodwaters drown a place that's always been dry. The Florida real estate bubble bursts. The real estate on Nag's Head falls into the sea. The question raised in these chapters is whether we can expose such truths before the deaths. Before the flood. Before the building collapse. Before the real-estate speculation spins out of control. That is the goal of scientists in their search for solutions. It is the goal of journalists as cogs in our creaky Democracy. And it is the goal of Fessmann and the other authors in this volume, a new generation of communicators becoming ever-more strategic for the good of people, the good of the Earth.

Contrary to Lee, facts exist. When harsh facts like those involving climate change are well-understood, we can protect ourselves, working on clean-energy plans, shoring up our coastlines, building resilience for future generations. When facts are suppressed, they come roaring at us in surprise; like Hurricane Michael, just short of Category 5, a storm that strengthened unusually rapidly before it devastated parts of the Florida Panhandle as this volume went to press -- a perfect storm for the history books.

References

Centopani, P. (2018, September 25). Nearly 700,000 properties damaged in the wake of Hurricane Florence. *National Mortgage News*

Crimmins, A. Balbus, B., Gamble, J. L., Beard, C. B., Bell, J. E., Dodgen, D., …, & Ziska, L. (2016). The impacts of climate change on human health in the United Staes: A scientific assessment. *U.S. Global Change Research Program*. DOI: 10.7930/J0R49NQX

Drye, W. (2018), *For sale – American paradise: How our nation was sold an impossible dream in Florida*. Guilford, CT: Lyons Press.

Fessmann, J. (2018a), "A Short History of Public Interest Communications," in *Fundamentals of Public Interest Communications* [Dissertation], University of Florida.

Fessmann. J. (2018). On communications war: Public interest communications and classical military strategy. *Journal of Public Interest Communications*, 2(1), 156-172. http://dx.doi.org/10.32473/jpic.v2.i1.p156

Lepore, J. (2018). *These truths: A history of the United States*. New York, NY: W.W. Norton.

Macnamara, J. (2016). The continuing convergence of journalism and PR: New Insights for ethical practice from a three-country study of senior practitioners. *Mass Communication Quarterly*, 93 (1),118–141. https://doi.org/10.1177/1077699015605803

Michaels, D. (2008). *Doubt is their product: How industry's assault on science threatens your health*. New York, NY: Oxford University Press.

Oreskes, N., & Conway, E. M. (2011). *Merchants of doubt: How a handful of scientists obscured the truth on issues from tobacco smoke to global warming.* London, UK: Bloomsbury.

Reed, K., Stansfield, A. M., Wehner, M. F., & Zarzycki, C.M. (2018, September 11). The human influence on hurricane Florence. Retrieved from https://cpb-us-e1.wpmucdn.com/you.stonybrook.edu/dist/4/945/files/2018/09/climate_change_Florence_0911201800Z_final-262u19i.pdf

Rachel Carson: A Conservation Legacy. (n.D.). *U.S. Fish & Wildlife Service.* Retrieved from www.fws.gov/rachelcarson/#bio.

Schneider, M. (2018, September 19). Report: PR pros outnumber journalists by a 6-to-1 ratio. *Ragan's PR Daily.*

Schwartz, J., & Fausset, R. (2018, September 12). North Carolina, warned of rising seas, chose to favor development. *The New York Times.* Retrieved from https://www.nytimes.com/2018/09/12/us/north-carolina-coast-hurricane.html

Editor's Introduction:
Climate Change Communications in the Age of Trump

Jasper Fessmann, PhD

Background and goal

The idea for this book emerged from a 2015 panel discussion at the University of Florida with Dr. Naomi Oreskes, eminent Professor of History of Science at Harvard University. The key insight gained from the debates with Naomi Oreskes and Cynthia Barnett was that journalists, climate activists and scientists are not usually trained in strategic communications but need to be. Currently, they are often outspent and outstrategized – and sometimes even unaware when they or their audiences are deliberately manipulated – by professional strategic communicators.

The book that has emerged here is not a comprehensive guide to climate change communications. Instead, it is a collection of spotlights on critical aspects of the issue with some roadmaps for specific approaches which each can have a direct impact on averting the looming global warming catastrophe through effective strategic communications.

It offers an overview of some of the most crucial issue in climate change communications and explores some specific areas where good public interest communications can move the needle on global warming. However, the book makes no claim to be comprehensive – unfortunately many areas and insights by great scholars and practitioners necessarily remained unexplored.

As a 20-year public relations veteran and educator, I see much of the global warming debate in the USA as a series of chess moves and countermoves in a communications war for public opinion. From this point of view, the climate change denial side is being very strategic and understands the rules, but unfortunately the public interest side often plays haphazard and without a strategy.

For most activists and scientists, this lack of strategy in communications is due to an overall lack of formal or informal communications training. In contrast, journalists are highly trained communicators but are not usually trained in strategic communications—this is seen as the domain of advocacy and public relations (PR) that they try to keep at arm's length. This means that at best, journalists' efforts to report on climate change and inspire action on solutions are limited to the tactical level.

Strategy defines long-term goals and the plan to achieve them—a roadmap for how to win a communications war (Fessmann, 2018). Tactics focus on individual engagements, specific plans, initiatives and specific parts of an issue. When tactics are not coordinated in accordance with strategy, they may have a short-term positive impact on long-term goals, but these gains may be offset when they are mismatched with other efforts at the tactical level. Uncoordinated tactics may even be harmful to the overall strategy. As the ancient Chinese General Sun Tzu (1910) put it, strategy without tactics is the slowest route to victory, but tactics without strategy is the noise before defeat.

A good example of tactics without strategy in climate communications is Al Gore's 2006 movie *An Inconvenient Truth*. It was tactically brilliant, inspiring millions of people and substantially raised awareness of the threat of global warming. However, strategically it lacked the follow through and planning to have a meaningful long-term impact on the global warming issue, increasing perceptions of threat without offering a roadmap forward. Because it was associated with a Democratic vice president, it played a large role in opening the door for professional climate change deniers to turn global warming into a conservative wedge issue and making the topic fully partisan. Just a few years after the release of *An Inconvenient Truth*, public acceptance of the dangers of global warming actually *decreased* and only returned to 2006-2007 levels in the late 2010s. Thus, the film was a brilliant tactical victory, but a strategic defeat because it helped to animate a highly effective climate change counter-movement (CCCM) which negatively influenced large segments of the general public in the United States.

The goal of this book, then, is to help journalists, advocates and scientists understand how the war for the public opinion is being fought at the strategic level and how they can become more resilient against the communications onslaughts by professional global warming denial communicators in their work. Additionally, this book aims to provide journalism and communications educators with classroom material to prepare the next generation of journalists and other storytellers to be able to spot and protect themselves from manipulation by strategically-trained PR professionals working for vested interests—even if the journalists themselves are wary of using strategy due to their professional credos.

Overview

This book deliberately mixes chapters by great work of climate communications practitioners with highly relevant peer-reviewed academic articles. The goal is to build a stronger bridge between academic researchers and the communicators in the trenches. The practitioner articles are relevant to academics; the peer-reviewed articles are relevant for non-academics. The chapters have been ordered to strengthen and support the respective professions, together telling a story about why climate change denial is so successful and how strategic, journalistic and educational techniques can be deployed to help improve the situation.

In the following I summarize each chapter in my own words to give the reader an overview and appreciation of the chapters:

Chapter 1: *An Unlevel Playing Field: A Primer on the Problems of Climate Change Communications* - Jasper Fessmann, PhD - This chapter serves as a primer on some key issues in climate change communications. It argues that much of the science reporting and climate change communications are stuck in an information-deficit model of trying to raise awareness, and to provide as much information as possible - in the vain hope that this will lead to positive social change. This has rarely worked for the last 30 years for reasons that are clear if considered from an economic perspective: The fossil fuel industry has a vital interest in protecting its business model worth trillions of dollars. This led them to invest up to a billion dollars a year in climate change denial organizations. The average of 900 million/year spend on climate change denial represents the equivalent of one-ninth, or 11% of the total revenues of all PR agencies in the USA combined. With so much money at their disposal, climate change deniers were able to hire some of the most highly trained, strategic PR professionals and researchers to wage their war on public opinion. Because of the imbalances in financial might and strategic expertise, these professional climate denial communicators won victory after victory and achieved their main goal of stymying meaningful change on global warming.

Chapter 2: *Turning Climate Misinformation into an Educational Opportunity* - John Cook, PhD - This peer-reviewed chapter shows how deliberate misinformation ("fake news") works and why it has been such a powerful tool to be wielded by professional climate change deniers: For example, the most shared social media article about climate change in 2016 described global warming to be a hoax. Furthermore, only 12% of Americans think that the scientific consensus on climate change is above 90%.

Turning the issue from a bi-partisan topic into a highly partisan, tribal wedge issue, misinformation lies at the heart of why climate change denial is such a problem in the United States. Based on the literature, Cook identifies five core climate disbeliefs: it's not happening, it's not us (not man-made), it's not bad, it's too hard to fix and an attack on the integrity of science. Cook shows that misinformation and falsehoods do damage by reducing perceived consensus and producing a polarizing effect, widening the gap between liberals and conservatives. Especially insidious is implicit misinformation, containing a mix of facts and falsehoods, such as false-balance media coverage, where climate scientists are given equal weight with contrarian voices. These false-balance presentations effectively cancel out the impact of accurate scientific information, and the misinformation does not even have to be coherent, evidence-based, or believable to reduce belief in facts.

Different types of misinformation require different responses. For example, informing people about the 97% scientific consensus can only be effective in countering the implicit misinformation of false-balance media coverage if it is not canceled out by explicit misinformation. Thus, simply communicating the facts is not enough to overcome explicit misinformation. Instead, Cook argues for an inoculation approach where the techniques used to distort facts are explained in order to neutralize explicit misinformation. Especially effective is "prebunking" misinformation – providing a "weak" dose of misinformation that the target has not yet been exposed to and then immediately debunking it to create immunity against this strain of inaccuracy. Such inoculation approaches can be used to counter the five core climate disbeliefs by describing the five characteristics of science denial as: fake experts, logical fallacies, impossible expectations, cherry picking and conspiracy theories (FLICC). Cook also discusses *misconception-based learning* as an effective teaching approach for climate change communications. Furthermore, he examines a technology-based fact-checking solution to counter fake news called "technocognition". Overall, Cook provides an in-depth scientific look at why professional climate deniers have been so successful in their impact on public opinion. However, Cook also offers effective ways in which understanding the misinformation mechanisms can be used for educational purposes to bolster audience resilience.

Chapter 3: *Intentional Circumvention: Navigating Around Denial and Towards Each Other* - Anthony Rogers-Wright - looks at ways to portray climate change that shifts from concept to mobilization, especially through storytelling. Crucially, the messaging needs to move from "No" (no more fossil fuels, no more carbon pollution, etc.) to getting to the *"Yes"* of embracing the necessary change. Using an Aikido analogy, Rogers-Wright argues that we need to channel the force of the aggression of the climate change deniers against them by *intentional circumvention* without exerting force ourselves. We must choose messages that are accessible and present solutions that offer a vision of the future we collectively want.

Rogers-Wright looks at the cultural and financial factors at play in the climate change debate and how we reached a situation where the news channel we watch is one of the best indicators of political and social affiliation. He also notes the crucial time disparity in climate narratives: The deniers have dominated the narratives for 40 years. We don't have that time – so we need effective shortcuts. However, he notes that *climate events,* such as hurricanes, haven't made good shortcuts because they don't lead to social change. He argues that a core problem in such communications is that *intersectionality* (the sense of shared suffering in spite of different specific consequences of climate change experienced) was ignored. Stories embracing *intersectionality,* in particular, those of the disproportionate impacts of the climate crisis on marginalized communities, specifically low-wealth communities and communities of color, can be powerful narratives often neglected in climate change communications. Climate change is as much about social injustice as about rising sea levels. To be effective, we need to build an inclusive movement that embraces visceral storytelling. Storytelling must be our primary method for injecting new urgency and bold ideas into confronting the intersecting crises of climate change, racism and inequality. As an example, Rogers-Wright describes his work in "RegeNErate Nebraska." The group aims at fostering agricultural transformation towards a regenerative model that focuses on soil health, ethical treatment of livestock and access to affordable, nutritious food.

Chapter 4: *Fire, Ice or Drought? Picturing Humanity in Climate Change Imagery* - Kim Sheehan, PhD, Nicole Dahmen, PhD and David Morris, PhD - This peer-reviewed chapter examines the role of visual communications such as the polar bear on a vanishing ice piece. It argues that pictures can sometimes transfer narratives and empathy even more powerful than words since pictures reach us on a visceral level. Pictures have the power to move audiences from complacency to action. While photographs of natural disasters linked to climate change and other "fear" based imagery have garnered attention and made the issue more prevalent, they are problematic because they also reduce efficacy (the sense of being able to do something about it) and thus hinder action.

This chapter uses an experiment to test the effectiveness of visual climate change messages. The chapter specifically looked at what type of climate change pictures (forest fire, melting ice, extreme drought) worked best and how the inclusion of people (no people, small group, individual), and locality of the climate effect (local or global) affected emotions and engagement. It found that having a single individual (vs. no person or group) in the picture was the most important personification effect of visual communication, especially if that person exemplified direct suffering from the climate effects (instead of a scientist talking about it). As far as the setting is concerned, forest fires resonated most strongly, likely because they relate directly to audiences' own experiences. Localization to the US does not seem to make much of a difference. Based on the evidence, from a strategic communications standpoint, we thus need to visually abandon the polar bear on the tiny ice block and replace the core climate change visual messaging with the suffering of real people, particularly suffering from the effects of forest fires.

Chapter 5: *Arcane and Hidden: The Challenge of State Public Utilities Commissions for Climate Change Communications* - Nancy LaPlaca, J.D. - This chapter points out that a truly important stakeholder in the climate debate, public utilities governed at the state level, receives almost no attention in climate change communications. State regulators, through state agencies called public utility commissions (PUCs), often determine the state's electricity mix, i.e. how much coal, natural gas, nuclear, solar, wind, energy efficiency and other resources are used to generate (or save) electricity for the state. In some states, PUCs even act as quasi-judicial agencies with complete authority to set electricity policy without oversight from the governor or state legislature. Dealing with the legally arcane and complex rules of PUCs requires uniquely qualified attorneys making it very hard for people working on climate change to promote policies that allow clean energy to thrive.

Given the importance of PUCs, the utility companies governed by them routinely spend millions of dollars on pay-to-play lobbying and sometimes resort to outright bribery. The arcane nature and complexness of PUC rules make the commissions difficult to understand, let alone explain to the general public. This issue is part of the reason why, for example, the "Sunshine State" of Florida, with up to 266 sunny days a year (in Fort Myers), uses only 0.31% solar.

Environmental interveners and policy experts at state PUCs must receive adequate strategic climate communications support to change the situation. With this, local citizens can be mobilized to take an interest in PUC decisions and become active in trying to stop bad policies and/or push for environmentally friendly ones. Organizers have used social media, intervened in dockets, showed up for hearings, and made their voices heard, for example against the Keystone Pipeline in Nebraska. Changing PUCs to reflect the climate change reality and making their membership more representative may be one of the most important actions to impact U.S. carbon emissions – and does not rely on changing the federal government.

Chapter 6: *Reframing the Narrative Around Solar Technology: Unlikely Opportunities for Bipartisanship in an Increasingly Divided Nation* - Ishana Ratan - This peer-reviewed chapter looks at how solar energy is framed in the public debate and how reframing solar stories could help expand the industry's potential, reducing greenhouse emissions. Eighty-nine percent of Americans support solar expansion and prices have dropped by 80% due to cheap mass-production developments in China in recent years. However, as Ratan notes, "key segments of the public are vulnerable to misleading narratives structured by conservative elites, while potential activists remain unengaged due to unfocused messaging from pro-trade and pro-solar organizations." US-based solar panel producers, for example, spin their decline in market share as unfair Chinese trade practices and find an open ear in the Trump Administration, forgetting the numerous cuts in subsidies and lack of domestic support that originally led to the loss of their competitive advantage.

From an economic standpoint, solar is a high technology intensive industry where economy of scale is an important competitive advantage. As Ratan notes, Chinese supply chains and efficient business model has rendered United States solar cell manufacturing a declining industry with little potential for future growth regardless of protectionist policy. While the manufacturing side has thus remained stagnant at around 30,000 jobs, the availability of cheap solar panels led to a dramatic rise in the downstream solar installation industry with over 137,000 jobs in 2016 (which is about three times the jobs left in the entire coal industry in the U.S.). Thus, there are two diverged job narratives at play: anecdotal stories about loss of the good old days in solar manufacturing on the one side and potentially stories of incredible growth in installation.

These narratives of loss of American manufacturing were picked up by Donald Trump, whose 2018 trade sanctions against China pose an existential threat to these jobs by potentially doubling the costs of solar panels which could result in the loss of over 88,000 jobs. These destructive narratives were not countered by collective action and counter-framing by the workers and firms in solar installation, despite the existential threat these narratives and resulting protectionist trade barriers pose to them. Ratan concludes that the divided media's portrayal of low skilled blue-collar workers engaged in a zero-sum economic struggle against liberal elites creates a false dichotomy between two groups who have the same common interest: economic prosperity and a greener future. However, if effective counter-narratives are employed, the impact of existing frames may be lessened over time, and the narrative balance shifted. The installation industry and environmental movement need to construct a cohesive, positive, bi-partisan narrative surrounding manufacturing, the solar industry, and domestic economic conditions that tailor the narrative to the intended audience in a way that personally connects them to the larger issues of protectionism and climate change.

Chapter 7: *Key Strategic Climate Denial Techniques Journalists Should Understand* - Jasper Fessmann, PhD - This chapter looks at how journalists can be manipulated by professional global warming deniers through the rhetoric of "activism" and "journalistic objectivity" to generate objectively false reporting. It discusses some counter strategies. Secondly, it looks at one particularly destructive group of climate change deniers: "Kooks," a nickname for former scientists who deny the scientific consensus because of their egos.

One of the most important strategies used by professional deniers was to attack the integrity of science in general, ruthlessly exploiting an inherent weakness in the scientific method. Recognizing the processes and need for climate change advocates and journalists to understand strategic communications is a critical step in countering the ongoing manipulation of the media and public opinion by the advocates for vested interests.

References

Fessmann. J. (2018). On communications war: Public interest communications and classical military strategy. *Journal of Public Interest Communications*, 2(1), 156-172. http://dx.doi.org/10.32473/jpic.v2.i1.p156

Tzu, S. (1910). *Sun Tzu and the art of war*. Lionel Giles (Trans.). (2000): Leicester, United Kingdom: Allandan Online Publishing.

Chapter 1

An Unlevel Playing Field:
A Primer on the Problems of Climate
Change Communications

Jasper Fessmann, PhD

"Gridlock is the greatest friend a global warming skeptic has, because that's all you really want. There's no legislation we're championing. We're the negative force. We're just trying to stop stuff. "

Marc Morano (Kenner & Robledo, 2014, 1:09:38-1:09:38:46).

Introduction

This chapter discusses, from a public interest communications perspective (PIC) (Fessmann, 2016, 2017, 2018a, 2018b), some of the core issues that have plagued climate change communications for a long time. It is intended to serve as a primer on the topic for non-specialists providing a simplified overview of the unique issues faced by climate change communications. As a practitioner chapter, I choose - for parsimony's sake - to omits acknowledgements/citations of a large number of significant contributions of many scholars working in the areas covered on which these insights are grounded in. I apologize to all those whose contributions I could not properly acknowledge here.

The chapter shows that most traditional climate change communications efforts operate on an information-deficit model of communications–trying to raise awareness of the problem and convince the public that change is necessary using factual evidence. While critical in the 1980s and early 1990s, this approach has become been less effective over the last 30 years, especially at influencing politically and economically powerful individuals who more easily shape change.

This chapter takes an economic view of many climate deniers as rational, self-interested *homo economicus* with clear incentives not to be convinced by scientific information alone. In doing so, it shows why it makes economic sense for the fossil fuel industry and allies to spend billions of dollars on climate denial. This public relations push on behalf of climate denial has successfully dominated the climate debate for decades, achieving the main goal of climate change denial: stymieing meaningful, systematic change on the climate issue and thus protecting trillions of dollars for the companies that operate in the status quo.

Stuck in an information-deficit model of communications

For almost forty years, climate scientists, journalists and activists have warned about the dangers of catastrophic climate change. While raising awareness of the issue was critical in the early days, the usefulness of this approach has continuously declined since the 1990s. It is simply no longer the case that the various publics have not heard about the danger of climate change. Instead, almost everyone has already formed some kind of opinion, often shaped by deliberately misguided information by professional climate change deniers.

A common fallacy of climate change communications is that raising awareness of the issues is sufficient to change minds, including the minds of influencers, about the dangers of climate change. This model is called an information-deficit approach. As the Oxford Research Encyclopedia of Climate Science describes it, the deficit model *"assumes that gaps between scientists and the public are a result of a lack of information or knowledge."* As a result, the information-deficit approach uses *"a one-way communication model where information flows from experts to publics in an effort to change individuals' attitudes, beliefs, or behaviors" (Suldovsky, 2017, par 1).*

However, there are problems with the information-deficit approach. It is extremely hard to change pre-existing opinions on important issues, or as David Ropeik (2010) put it *"our opinions are castle walls, built to keep us safe"* (par 1). This arises partly because of the deep discomfort most people feel at the revelation of new facts that contradict their existing opinions and attitudes. This discomfort is called *cognitive dissonance* (Festinger, 1957). Because it is psychologically uncomfortable to hold two conflicting ideas or beliefs at the same time, people work psychologically to resolve this discomfort by resisting the new information. Two common tools used to resist new facts are *selective exposure*—deliberately avoiding news sources of potential challenging information (Klapper, 1960)—and *confirmation bias*—only seeking out and viewing facts that are supportive of the original worldview as credible (Wason, 1960).

As a result of the challenges associated with changing opinions, influence/awareness campaigns work best if the audience does not yet have a strong opinion on the issue to begin with. If the campaign is successful, the audience will adopt the campaign's position and defend it, regardless of the objective merits of the original message. Because climate change is a politically polarized issue that most people already have an opinion on, awareness-raising campaigns will not be as effective.

This understanding leads the field of public interest communications (PIC) to posit that awareness is a pre-condition for political and social change but does not automatically lead to change. PIC is broadly defined as *"science-based strategic communications to advance the human condition"* (Fessmann, 2018b, p. 138). More specifically:

> *Public interest communications is the development and implementation of science based, planned strategic communication campaigns with the main goal of achieving significant and sustained positive behavioral change on a public interest issue that transcends the particular interests of any single organization.* (Fessmann, 2016, p. 16)

From a PIC activism point of view, many climate change communications efforts lack focus on the kinds of crystal-clear call-to-actions that lead to sustained behavioral change. Although awareness campaigns may still impact children and young adults who have not fully formed opinions on climate change, they will be less effective for broader segments of the population, and particularly ineffective on political conservatives who already have strong opinions on the issue.

An economic view of climate change denial

A core assumption of information-deficit model approach is that targeted publics are ignorant of the facts and that if enough facts are provided, people will accept the data suggesting that anthropogenic climate change presents a dire threat for the survival of the human species. This viewpoint presupposes that humans are ultimately rational actors planning for long-term changes and as such will take the course of action best for the species. However, economics presents an alternative perspective on climate change that can be understood as rational. Understanding why people—particularly influencers who have the potential to make major changes in policy and business—believe they are making a rational case for denying climate change is critical to understanding how to address the problem.

This economical approach treats most climate change deniers as *homo economicus* ("economic man"), or rational actors pursuing wealth for their own self-interest (Rodriguez-Sickert, 2009). Deniers have self-interested reasons for climate change denial that appear rational to them. To bypass this, financial and cultural incentives must be changed.

Accepting the dangers of climate change as real requires significant changes to existing business models and operational structures. Today's managers, businesspeople, and policymakers may safely assume that the most extreme effects of climate change will not directly affect them. However, the costs to their business associated with addressing climate change do have an immediate and possibly negative effect on their economic situation. Thus, denying climate change is a way to protect their current perceived interests.

Compounding deniers' motivation to protect their current interests is that the most catastrophic consequences of climate change are likely to be experienced in the future. Humans routinely engage in what behavioral economist call *temporal discounting* (Frederick, Loewenstein, & O'Donoghue, 2002), placing less value on possible benefits or outcomes that take longer to appear. While there may be long-term benefits for companies and economies in making such adjustments, these benefits are not immediately visible to those accustomed to the timeframe of business quarterly financial reporting or election cycles.

These economic factors illustrate why campaigns focusing on reducing ignorance about climate change and focusing on benefits to the future can be unpersuasive for many key decision-makers, and why they may feel incentivized to support climate change counter-movements (CCCM). Consider the case of Exxon. As Banerjee, Song, and Hasemyer (2015) describe in their award-winning expose, "Exxon: The road not taken," Exxon was on the leading edge of climate science in the late 1970s and early 1980s and among the first to realize the dangers of climate change. Accepting such data, however, required fossil fuel executives to make a choice: either inform the public and radically change their business model to become leading alternative energy companies or maintain their existing, highly profitable fossil fuel business model. The existing model worked well with minimal investment, while changing the model would have meant restructuring and heavy investment in untried technologies. Furthermore, company leaders tend to earn performance bonuses based on the company's short-term gains, meaning that business model changes could have a real and personal financial impact on leaders. From a *homo economics* point of view, then, fossil fuel company managers acted rationally by opting to optimize their personal wealth optimization despite the negative consequences to the environment.

The climate denial communications industry

With billions of dollars in the game, it is not surprising that some very effective but amoral communications strategists operated in climate change denial realm and that a whole shadow communications industry has emerged. This is best exemplified by Marc Morano, named Climate Change Misinformer of the Year 2011 by Media Matters for America, which described him as *"the Matt Drudge of climate denial," the "king of the skeptics," and "a central cell of the climate-denial machine"* (Thee, & Fitzsimmons, 2012, para 1). Without any formal scientific training, Morano *"is adamant that manmade global warming is a 'con job' based on 'subprime science'"* and that climate change is a *"hoax"* (para 1).

Morano originally was a door-to-door salesman and conservative activist, who started his communications career working for Rush Limbaugh and Sen. James Inhofe (R-OK). During the 2004 U.S. presidential campaign, he was first to publish the blatantly false claims by Vietnam swift-boat veterans that Democratic presidential nominee Senator John Kerry had embellished and lied about his war record (Kaufman, 2009). The campaign ads by the so-called *Swift Boat Veterans for Truth* by a Bush aligned Super PAC managed to successfully destroy John Kerry's key presidential campaign narrative as war hero even before the Democratic National Convention. Kerry's inability to recognize this fact and change his strategy played a crucial role in his electoral defeat. As the New Yorker Magazine described it: John Kerry *"was defined and thereafter demolished by a masterful if venal tag-team consisting of the Bush campaign and the proto-super PAC Swift Boat Veterans for Truth"* (Drapper, 2012, para 37).

Besides, the obvious effectiveness of Swift Boat Veterans for Truth, the campaign exhibited another feature that recommended it to potential emulators: it was extremely cost-effective. The campaign showed clearly that *"ruthless, relentless storytelling could be done on the cheap"* (Drapper, 2012, para 37).

From an amoral strategic communications standpoint, Morano is an example of a ruthlessly brilliant communicator embodying a warfighting mentality (Fessmann, 2018). Marc Morano is very open about his role and even revels in it: *"You can't be afraid of the absolute hand-to-hand combat, metaphorically, and you got to name names and go after the individuals, you can't go just after a system... what I enjoy the most is going after the individual because that is where something lives or dies"* (Kenner & Robledo, 2014, 1:04:45-1:05:00).

Part of the problem here is that the general public and many journalists view climate change denial NGO's as well-meaning and activist-staffed as most other NGO's. There is an inherent assumption of a do-gooder organization which may be a bit whacky such as the Flat Earth Society but overall made up by enthusiasts. While there are true believers in the climate change denial movement, it is critical that journalists and the public realize that is also a billion-dollar industry strategically lead by highly professional communicators.

Global warming denial as a crisis management strategy

The scientific and public pressure for meaningful action on global warming starting in the 1980s posed an existential threat for fossil fuel interests and their allies. As such, from a crisis management perspective, climate change denial was a highly effective strategic communications countermeasure that preserved the status quo for the next 40 years. Illuminatingly, the British political comedy "Yes, Prime Minister" in the 1980s described a four-stage crisis response strategy (Jay & Lynn, 1986) that fits well the observed communication efforts of global warming deniers since:

1) Say nothing is going to happen.

2) Say something may be about to happen, but nothing should be done about it.

3) Say that maybe we should do something about it, but there's nothing we currently *can* do.

4) Say maybe there was something we could have done, but unfortunately, it's too late now.

In the last 30-40 years, the first stage of the response communications strategy has been dominant but there are indications that the later stages now become more prevalent. This phenomenon however requires further study and is beyond the scope of this chapter. The central strategy in stage 1 was to create as much doubt as possible on the science of climate change. By doing so, climate deniers provided people with a vested economic or social reason for denying climate change with a psychological coping mechanism to reduce the cognitive dissonance generated by new scientific information. Campaigns would, for example, posit that "the science is not in yet" about climate change to provide audiences with an alternative interpretation of climate change that does not require behavioral change. This strategy can be quite effective: as leading CCCM strategic communicator Marc Morano put it: *"Gridlock is the greatest friend a global warming skeptic has, because that's all you really want. There's no legislation we're championing. We're the negative force. We're just trying to stop stuff."*(Kenner & Robledo, 2014, 1:09:38-1:09:38:46).

The financial backing of industry and conservative allies was critical in creating public gridlock. For example, Brulle (2014) showed that between 2003–2010, 91 denialist non-governmental organizations (NGOs) raised combined revenues of more than $7.26 billion dollars—an average of more than $900 million per year. To put this into perspective, the total of American PR agency revenues for the same period was $65.85 billion (Statista.com A, 2018). This means that climate denial organizations received the equivalent of 11% (one-ninth) of total PR agency spending in the entire United States.

This is in addition to lobbying money spend on behalf of the oil and gas industry: In 2017, the oil and gas industry was ranked 4th in total money spent on lobbying at all levels of government in the USA (Statista.com B, 2018). The lobbying power of the oil and gas industry is well understood by journalists and most of the public. For example, in 2003, the oil and gas industry spent $57 million dollars on their official lobbying work (OpenSecret.org, 2018) and this bought them a lot of influence on energy decisions on every governmental level. Striking however is how little money this is if contrasted with the indirect CCCM spending: the total oil and gas industry lobbying effort is a mere 6,2% of the average $900 million/year spend on global warming denial. This means that up to 20 times more money may have been spent on climate change denial through the indirect, often secret, CCCM channels than the oil/gas industry spend on their direct lobbying efforts.

Further complicating the issue is that hundreds of millions of dollars of CCCM's income are *black money*, meaning the donors were not disclosed (Brulle, 2014). This could allow oil companies to spend a token amount on pro-global warming advocacy as a PR stunt while spending hundreds of times more to continue denial through secretive channels without the public knowing about it. This may become a more attractive option for them as public pressures force more and more fossil fuel companies to at least publicly accept the scientific consensus on man-made climate change.

As a PR strategy, paying for a token campaign or pseudo-event for publicity while perpetuating policies harmful to the public interest would be nothing new. For decades cigarette companies spend token money on so-called *youth prevention campaigns* which had no positive impact on reducing teen smoking (HHS, 2012) while at the same time spending hundred times more on advertising specifically targeting youth *"starters"* (Pollay, 2000), influencing children as young as age 3 (Fischer, Schwartz, Richards, Goldstein, & Rojas, 1991).

By 2018, most major fossil fuel companies have publicly acknowledged the reality of global warming and some have even pledged action. For example, in September 2018, Exxon Mobil announced it would spend $1 million over two years to support a Republican-led lobbying effort for a US carbon tax (Irfan, 2018). However, the proposal supported would also grant oil companies immunity from future climate lawsuits (Irfan, 2018). In comparison, the 1998 Tobacco Master Settlement Agreement (MSA) which granted immunity from lawsuits for the tobacco industry stipulated a minimum payment of $206 billion USD over 25 years by the top four tobacco companies (NAAG, 1998).

Given Exxon's potential legal exposure regarding climate denial, this effort, if successful, would be a great win for them at a bargain price.

The 500.000$/year spent by Exxon on lobbying for a carbon tax represents just 0.42% of the 120 million dollars spent by the oil and gas industry on their lobbying efforts in 2017 (Statista.com B, 2018). Exxon advocacy effort represents a 1/2400th of the 1.2 billion dollars of CCCM revenues in 2010 (Brulle, 2014). If CCCM spending continued unabated, Exxon's pro-climate change contribution would be outmatched 2000+ times on the other side - to use an idiom, it's *a drop in the ocean* of the money involved in climate change communications. Even if the fossil fuel industry would fully cease CCCM support, it is not clear how much of an impact that would have now. While early fossil fuel industry support may have been critical to the development of CCCMs, the climate change counter-movement has long since become a self-perpetuating conservative ideological movement with a momentum that most likely will keep on going even without direct industry support.

Oil companies pushing specifically for a carbon tax may also be problematic in general. Carbon taxes have long been very unpopular - until 2016 support in the general public never registered above 36% and only 15% of Republicans supported a carbon tax (Carbon Tax Center, 2018), although the support for a carbon tax has since gone up across all demographics. Thus, pushing for a carbon tax may have the opposite effect of the official intention: increasing global warming denial by reinforcing it as a political wedge issue among conservatives who don't favor new taxes anyway. The data on this is not clear yet, and it would benefit from further research, but the nature of the issues raises the possibility of ruthless exploitation of the scientific data for purposes of PR campaigns deliberately designed to harm the public interest, while at the same time increase a company's public image.

As of now, there are no whistleblower accounts showing that oil companies deliberately chose advocacy for carbon taxes knowing of the potentially opposite effect. However, from a PR perspective using token campaigns precisely because they have the opposite effect is an amoral but highly effective communications strategy that has been used in the past. For example, tobacco companies spend millions on campaigns for parents to talk to their children about smoking (Sussman, 2002). They did this despite research clearly showing that these advertisements actually increased teenage smoking (Wakefield et al., 2006). Given the tobacco industry's strong focus on researched based advertising and PR decision making since the 1950's (Brandt, 2012), it is not surprising that the industry deliberately chose such type of campaigns precisely because they had the opposite effects of their official purpose, as internal documents about tobacco companies sophisticated use of research seem to indicated (Pollay, 2000).

Conclusion

This chapter explores how and why raising awareness of climate change as part of an information-deficit model approach is not effective at achieving sustained, meaningful social change to counter the existential threat posed by global warming. It offers a different way of looking at the reasons why global warming denial is logical from an economic/behavioral economic point of view. Understanding the motives and incentives behind global warming denial identifies which social, cultural, and economic incentives need to be changed to make global warming communications more effective in generating behavior change.

While climate change communicators and scientist have long learned that they are financially not on a level playing field, a deep analysis shows the full extent of the power imbalance: around 900 million USD are spent annually by global warming denial organizations representing the equivalent of 1/9th of the total expenditure on public relations in the United States. These figures are mindboggling but were dwarfed by the trillions of dollars the fossil fuel industries and other vested interest successfully reaped by slowing down meaningful change on the global warming issue.

From a PIC standpoint, the sad truth is that despite many valiant efforts of climate scientist, activists, and journalist over the course of the last 40 years the vested interest fighting a communications war to preserve their business models resoundingly achieved their main goal – global warming gridlock and the continued dependence on a fossil fuel-based economy.

The battle so far was activists David without an effective weapon vs. fully armored and superbly equipped corporate vested interests Goliath. However, once journalist and activists develop a deeper understanding of strategic public interest communications, David may have a sharp communications stone in his sling that, if targeted accurately, can smite the mightiest CCCM Goliath.

References

Banerjee, N., Song, L., & Hasemyer, D. (2015, September 16): Exxon: The road not taken - Exxon's own research confirmed fossil fuels' role in global warming decades ago. *Inside Climate News*. Retrieved from https://insideclimatenews.org/content/Exxon-The-Road-Not-Taken

Brandt, A.M. (2012). Inventing conflicts of interest: A history of tobacco industry tactics. *American Journal of Public Health, 102*(1), 63-71.

Brulle, R. J. (2014). Institutionalizing delay: Foundation funding and the creation of U.S. climate change counter-movement organizations. *Climatic change, 122*(4), 681–694. doi:10.1007/s10584-013-1018-7

Carbon Tax Center (2018, August). *Polls*. Retrieved from https://www.carbontax.org/polls/

Draper, R. (2012, July 5). *Can the Democrats catch up in the Super-PAC game?* The New York Times Magazine. Retrieved from https://www.nytimes.com/2012/07/08/magazine/can-the-democrats-catch-up-in-the-super-pac-game.html?ref=magazine

Fessmann. J. (2016). The emerging field of public interest communications. In E. Oliveira, A. D. Melo & G. Goncalves (Eds.). *Strategic communication in non-profit organizations: Challenges and alternative approaches* (pp. 13-34). Wilmington: Vernon Press.

Fessmann, J., (2017). Conceptual foundations of public interest communications. *Journal of Public Interest Communications, 1*(1), 16-30. http://dx.doi.org/10.32473/jpic.v1.i1.p16

Fessmann. J. (2018a). On communications war: Public interest communications and classical military strategy. *Journal of Public Interest Communications, 2*(1), 156-172. http://dx.doi.org/10.32473/jpic.v2.i1.p156

Fessmann. J. (2018b). *Fundamentals of public interest communications* [Dissertation]. University of Florida.

Festinger, L. (1957). *A theory of cognitive dissonance.* Evanston, Ill: Row, Peterson.

Fischer, P. M., Schwartz, M. P., Richards, J. W., Goldstein, A. O., & Rojas, T. H. (1991). Brand logo recognition by children aged 3 to 6 years Mickey Mouse and Old Joe the Camel. *JAMA, 266*(22), 3145–3148. doi:10.1001/jama.1991.03470220061027

Frederick, S., Loewenstein, G., & O'Donoghue, T. (2002). Time discounting and time preference: A critical review. *Journal of Economic Literature, 40*, 351-401.

HHS - U.S. Department of Health and Human Services (2012). *Preventing Tobacco Use Among Youth and Young Adults: A Report of the Surgeon General.* Atlanta, GA: HHS, U.S. Centers for Disease Control and Prevention (CDC), National Center for Chronic Disease Prevention and Health Promotion, Office on Smoking and Health.

Irfan, U. (2018, October 18). Exxon is lobbying for a carbon tax. There is, obviously, a catch. *Vox.* Retrieved from https://www.vox.com/2018/10/18/17983866/climate-change-exxon-carbon-tax-lawsuit

Jay, A. & Lynn, J. (Writers), Lotterby, S. (Producer). (1986, February 13). A victory for democracy [Television series episode]. In Allen, S., Lotterby, S., & Whitmore, P. (Producers). *Yes, Prime Minister.* London, UK: BBC Two.

Kaufman, L. (2009, April 9). Dissenter on warming expands his campaign. *The New York Times.* Retrieved from https://www.nytimes.com/2009/04/10/us/politics/10morano.html

Kenner, R. & Robledo, M. [Producer], Kenner, R. [Director]. (2014). *Merchants of Doubt* [Motion Picture]. United States: Sony Pictures Classics

Klapper, J. T. (1960). *The effects of mass communication.* Glencoe, Ill: Free Press.

NAAG (1998). Master Settlement Agreement. Retrieved from http://www.naag.org/backpages/naag/tobacco/msa/msa-pdf/1109185724_1032468605_cigmsa.pdf

OpenSecretes.org (n.d.). Industry Profile: Summary, 2003. Retrieved from https://www.opensecrets.org/lobby/indusclient.php?id=E01&year=2003

Pollay, R.W. (2000). Targeting youth and concerned smokers: Evidence from Canadian tobacco industry documents. *Tobacco Control, 9,* 136-147.

Rodriguez-Sickert, C. (2009). Homo economicus. In J. Peil & I. van Staveren (Eds.), *Handbook of economics and ethics* (pp. 223-229). Northampton, MA: Edward Elgar Publishing

Ropeik, David (2010, July 13). Why changing somebody's mind, or yours, is hard to do. *Psychology Today.* Retrieved from https://www.psychologytoday.com/us/blog/how-risky-is-it-really/201007/why-changing-somebody-s-mind-or-yours-is-hard-do

Statista.com A (2018). Estimated aggregate revenue of U.S. public relations agencies from 2000 to 2016 (in billion U.S. dollars). Retrieved from https://www.statista.com/statistics/183972/estimated-revenue-of-us-public-relations-agencies-since-2000/

Statista.com B (2018). Top lobbying industries in the United States in 2017, by total lobbying spending (in million U.S. dollars). Retrieved from https://www.statista.com/statistics/257364/top-lobbying-industries-in-the-us/

Suldovsky, B. (2017). The information deficit model and climate change communication. *Oxford Research Encyclopedia of Climate Science.* Retrieved from http://climatescience.oxfordre.com/view/10.1093/acrefore/978019 0228620.001.0001/acrefore-9780190228620-e-301

Sussman, S. (2002). Tobacco industry youth tobacco prevention programming: A review. *Prevention Science, 3*(1), 57–67.

Thee, S., & Fitzsimmons, J. (2012, December 27). Climate change misinformer of the year: Marc Morano. *Media Matters for America.* Retrieved from https://www.mediamatters.org/research/2012/12/27/climate-change-misinformer-of-the-year-marc-mor/191878.

Wakefield, M., Terry-McElrath, Y., Emery, S., Saffer, H., Chaloupka, F. J., Szczypka, G., Flay, B., O'Malley, P. M., … Johnston, L. D. (2006). Effect of televised, tobacco company-funded smoking prevention advertising on youth smoking-related beliefs, intentions, and behavior. *American Journal of Public Health, 96*(12), 2154-60.

Wason, P. C. (1960). On the failure to eliminate hypotheses in a conceptual task. *Quarterly Journal of Experimental Psychology, 12* (3), 129–40. doi:10.1080/17470216008416717

Chapter 2

Turning Climate Misinformation into an Educational Opportunity

John Cook, PhD

Introduction

"Education is a better safeguard of liberty than a standing army."

Edward Everett

Misinformation is information that is initially presented as true but later found to be false (Lewandowsky, Ecker, Seifert, Schwarz, & Cook, 2012). Misinformation can prevent the public from learning correct facts, which in turn can lead to public preferences different to those if they had been accurately informed (Kuklinski, Quirk, Jerit, Schwieder, & Rich, 2000). Such outcomes can have significant consequences for democracy, which requires a well-informed populace to properly function.

Misinformation as a societal issue has become particularly prevalent in recent years. In 2014, online misinformation was named one of the top ten global trends of concern (World Economic Forum, 2014). Oxford Dictionary named "post-truth" the word of the year in 2016 (Flood, 2016). The 2016 U.S. election marked an elevation in the salience of misinformation and fake news. Politifact assessed that 68% of Donald Trump's statements were false although this low performance did not prevent his electoral victory (Politifact, 2017). One analysis found that President Donald Trump made 492 false or misleading claims in the first 100 days of his presidency (Washington Post, 2017).

Misinformation associated with the 2016 election also originated from a range of sources beyond the Presidential candidate. Bessi and Ferrara (2016) found that one-fifth of online conversation during the U.S. election was generated by automatic social media bots, with 75% of the bots supportive of Donald Trump. Bots were retweeted as often as humans, indicating that users have trouble distinguishing between bots and humans (or don't care). Consistent with these results, Kollanyi, Howard, and Woolley (2016) found that Pro-Trump bots were around four times more prolific than pro-Clinton bots.

Misinformation is also highly relevant to the issue of climate change. An analysis of social media activity in 2016 found that the most shared article about climate change was an article claiming that climate change was a hoax (Readfearn, 2016). Boussalis and Coan (2016) found that in recent years, misinformation targeting climate science has been on the increase relative to arguments targeting climate policy. In posing the question "is the era of climate denial over?", the authors conclude unfortunately not.

However, the presence of climate misinformation dates back to the early 1990s and has had a significant influence on public discussion, public levels of climate literacy and climate policy for decades (McCright & Dunlap, 2000). Correspondingly, a large body of research has examined the phenomenon of climate science denial, analyzed the structure and techniques of misinformation, and experimentally tested interventions designed to neutralize its influence.

Research into misinformation is more relevant than ever in this current post-truth era. It can help us understand the various psychological impacts of misinformation and offer insights into evidence-based responses that can potentially reduce the influence of misinformation. Crucially, it points to ways that misinformation can be used for educational purposes, by increasing climate literacy and critical thinking skills.

Understanding climate misinformation

Misconceptions about climate change are numerous, which is to be expected given the complexity of our climate. Students hold a number of misconceptions about the causes of climate change and the greenhouse effect (Chang & Pascua, 2015; Gautier, Deutsch, & Rebich, 2006). Nearly half of U.S. teenagers believe that stopping rockets from punching holes in the ozone layer would reduce global warming (Leiserowitz, Smith, & Marlon, 2011). An international survey of adults found that one-third of adults think the Earth would be warmer with no greenhouse gases (Thompson, 2017). These misunderstandings are particularly consequential given the important role that understanding the greenhouse mechanism plays in acceptance of human-caused global warming (Ranney & Clark, 2016).

An especially damaging misconception is the lack of awareness of the high level of agreement among climate scientists that humans are causing global warming. Despite the fact that between 90 to 100% of climate scientists agree that humans are causing global warming (Cook et al., 2016), with a number of studies converging on 97% agreement (Anderegg, Prall, Harold, & Schneider, 2010; Cook et al., 2013; Doran & Zimmerman, 2009; Carlton, Perry-Hill, Huber, &

Prokopy, 2015), only 12% of Americans think that the scientific consensus is above 90% (Leiserowitz, Maibach, Roser-Renouf, Rosenthal, & Cutler, 2017). The discrepancy between public perception and the overwhelming scientific agreement is known as the "consensus gap". This gap varies across political ideology, with liberals showing higher perceived consensus relative to conservatives, indicating a strong influence of political ideology on climate perceptions.

In a meta-analysis of 25 polls and 171 academic studies across 56 nations, Hornsey, Harris, Bain, and Fielding (2016) found that the strongest predictors of climate beliefs were political affiliation and political ideology. One way that political ideology influences attitudes regarding climate change is through aversion to climate solutions. For example, when climate change information was presented with two different solutions to climate change (regulation of pollution or nuclear energy), political conservatives responded positively to the nuclear energy message but negatively to the regulation message (Campbell & Kay, 2014). Climate change information that was perceived to conflict with a person's ideology resulted in reduced acceptance of climate change.

In the case of Donald Trump, the underlying dynamic of economic beliefs driving scientific views is made explicit: the subtext becomes text. In a New York Times interview, Trump indicated his views on humanity's role in driving climate change was based to some degree on whether climate policy was economically viable (New York Times, 2016):

> *...I think there is some connectivity [between climate change and human activities]. [...] It depends on how much. It also depends on how much it's going to cost our companies.* (par 85)

While the consensus gap may be greater for conservatives, it still exists at the liberal end of the political spectrum. This indicates that misinformation, as well as a lack of awareness, also plays a part in public misconceptions about climate change. The misinformation campaign against climate change began to take form in the early 1990s, created by conservative think-tanks whose goal was to undermine the Kyoto Protocol (McCright & Dunlap, 2000). Rather than advocate alternative policies to mitigate climate change, the think-tanks began to cast doubt on the scientific evidence that necessitated mitigation policies. These efforts turned a bipartisan issue, with George H. W. Bush pledging to "fight the greenhouse effect with the White House effect" (Peterson, 1989, p. A1), into a polarized public debate. The fossil fuel industry was an ally and funder of the conservative misinformation campaign (Jacques, Dunlap, & Freeman, 2008; Farrell, 2015). From 2003 to 2010, 91 organizations known to disseminate climate misinformation received corporate funding totaling over $900 million per year (Brulle, 2014).

Misinformation is disseminated in a number of ways. Conservative think-tanks have been prolific in publishing a number of environmentally-skeptical books, most since 1992 (Jacques, Dunlap, & Freeman, 2008). Accompanying this strategy has been the exploitation of the journalistic norm of balanced media coverage of political issues. This has resulted in false-balance coverage of climate change (Painter & Ashe, 2012), which has been observed to reduce public perception of scientific consensus, thus widening the consensus gap (Cook, Lewandowsky, & Ecker, 2017).

The internet and social media are particularly effective in indiscriminately facilitating the spread of misinformation. Qiu, Oliveira, Shirazi, Flammini, and Menczer (2017) found that low quality information received just as many Facebook shares as high-quality information. Similarly, Weng, Flammini, Vespignani, and Menczer (2012) found that content quality was not a requisite for tweets to go viral. Social media has also led to the development of echo-chambers, accelerating the polarization of views on climate change (Jasny, Waggle, & Fisher, 2015). One danger of echo-chambers is the perception among climate science denialists that their views are widely shared, which renders them particularly resistant to changing their beliefs (Leviston et al., 2013).

The fracturing of the media landscape has also made it possible for politicians to target core constituents in a way that facilitates strategic political extremism (Glaeser, Ponzetto, & Shapiro, 2005). The interface between misinformation and political elites is a crucially important component in understanding the mechanisms by which misinformation influences the general public. From 1993 to 2003, the semantic similarity between climate misinformation, news media coverage, and U.S. Presidential statements increased, indicating a growing influence of climate misinformation (Farrell, 2016). Meta-analysis of public surveys found that cues from political elites are one of the most important drivers of public concern over global climate change (Carmichael & Brulle, 2017). Further, Mildenberger and Leiserowitz (2017) found that changes in political elite cues drove a reduction in acceptance of climate change in the late 2000s, rather than changes in economic conditions. This means that events such as Republican senators unanimously voting that humans aren't causing global warming (Kollipara, 2015) have real influence on Republican voters' views on climate change.

Political elites also influence climate policy in more direct ways. Other national leaders who were skeptical about human-caused global warming, such as President George W. Bush, Prime Minister Tony Abbott in Australia and Prime Minister Steve Harper in Canada, employed a number of strategies to delay climate change policies (De Pryck & Gemenne, 2017). These included appointing climate science denialists at the head of scientific agencies, abolishing advisory panels and scientific programs, cutting funding to environment portfolios, reorienting research towards more industry-relevant research, and censorship of federal scientists. Similar activities have been observed in the early stages of the Trump administration.

This body of research shows that climate misinformation has significant consequences on public attitudes and policy outcomes. In order to counter the negative impact of climate misinformation, a better understanding of the structure of climate misinformation, as well as its psychological impact, is required.

The five climate disbeliefs

Psychologists have identified five key beliefs regarding climate change (Ding, Maibach, Zhao, Roser-Renouf, & Leiserowitz, 2011): global warming is real, human activity is the primary cause, the impacts are bad, the experts agree on these first three points, and there's hope that we can avoid the worst impacts of climate change. A number of studies have examined different aspects of contrarian claims that argue against the mainstream positions of climate science. All contrarian arguments about climate change can be grouped under five denialist categories: it's not real, it's not us, it's not bad, the experts are unreliable, and there's no hope (i.e., climate solutions won't work). Mirroring the five climate beliefs, these denialist categories can be characterized the five climate disbeliefs.

An overview of analyses categorizing climate misinformation illustrates how individual studies tend to cover subsets of the five climate disbeliefs. Capstick and Pidgeon (2014) categorized two types of climate skepticism: epistemic (related to climate science) and response (related to climate solutions). Restricting his analysis to epistemic skepticism, Rahmstorf (2004) divided skeptic arguments into three categories: trend (it's not real), attribution (it's not us) and impact (it's not bad). Measuring people's beliefs in Rahmstorf's three types of skepticism, Poortinga et al. (2011) found that people who were skeptical about one aspect of climate change (e.g., whether humans were causing climate change) were more likely to be skeptical about other aspects of climate change (e.g., whether climate impacts would be serious). Akter, Bennett, and Ward (2012) found that skepticism about the human contribution to global warming was at the core of climate change skepticism, being a common source of impact and mitigation skepticism.

Mazo (2013) listed four stages of climate change denial encompassing both epistemic and response skepticism: it's not happening, it's not us, it's not bad, and it's too hard to fix. In addition to scientific or policy related claims, a fifth category focuses on attacking the integrity of climate science. An analysis of early conservative think-tank publications by McCright and Dunlap (2000) found that in addition to casting doubt on climate impacts and the efficacy of climate policies, a third key counter-claim questioned the strength of the scientific evidence for global warming. Machine learning analysis of conservative think-tank articles found that as well as policy and science arguments, a major theme was attacks on scientific integrity (Boussalis & Coan, 2016). Religious metaphors have been used in order to frame climate science as an unfounded belief (Nerlich, 2010; Woods, Fernandez, & Coen, 2010).

In summation, a number of studies have examined specific subsets of climate misinformation. An overarching framework encompassing all these studies finds that climate skepticism or denial can be summarized by five key disbeliefs. Since 2011, Donald Trump has expressed views on climate change spanning the five climate disbeliefs, mostly in the form of tweets (Matthews, 2017). Most of his utterances fall under the category that global warming isn't happening, typically in response to a cold weather event (Trump, 2013b). While people's views on the reality of global warming are subconsciously influenced by local temperature variations (Joireman, Truelove, & Duell, 2010; Li, Johnson, & Zaval, 2011), Trump's knee-jerk reaction to cold weather events are another stark example of subtext becoming text.

Further, Trump has argued that humans are not causing global warming (Trump, 2014a) and minimized the impacts (Trump, 2014b). On climate solutions, Trump has argued against renewable power (Trump, 2012a) and climate policy (Trump, 2013a). In casting doubt on the integrity of climate science, Trump famously characterized climate change as a conspiratorial hoax (Trump, 2012b).

Whether it be in tweets, public statements, media coverage or other mediums, misinformation about climate change influences people's views in a number of ways. Understanding the psychological mechanisms by which different types of misinformation does damage is key to developing interventions that neutralize its influence.

How misinformation does damage

Cook, Lewandowsky, and Ecker (2017) tested two types of misinformation: explicit and implicit. Explicit misinformation states outright falsehoods. The immediate impact of explicit misinformation is causing people to believe in false information. For example, exposing people to misinformation about the scientific consensus on climate change lowers perceived consensus (Cook et al., 2017; van der Linden, Leiserowitz, Rosenthal, & Maibach, 2017). Similarly, Ranney and Clark (2016) found that a few misleading statistics can reduce acceptance of climate change. Misinformation about climate change (both implicit and explicit) has also been found to disproportionately influence political conservatives (Cook et al., 2017; van der Linden et al., 2017). This means that climate misinformation has a polarizing effect, widening the gap between liberals and conservatives.

Implicit misinformation differs from explicit information in that it contains a mix of facts and falsehoods. A common form of implicit misinformation is false-balance media coverage, where climate scientists are given equal weight with contrarian voices. This has a more insidious influence than explicit misinformation but still has the result of significantly lowering perceived consensus (Cook et al., 2017). Other studies have found that false-balance presentations are effective in cancelling out the impact of accurate scientific information (McCright, Charters, Dentzman, & Dietz, 2016; van der Linden et al., 2017). Given the damaging impact of false-balance media coverage, it was of particular concern that the Trump administration at one time planned to conduct red versus blue team debates on climate science (Davidson & McNutt, 2017).

This research into implicit misinformation underscores the insidious danger of misinformation and fake news: it does not need to be coherent, evidence-based, or even believable. Without needing to convince people, misinformation can reduce belief in facts. When people are unable to resolve conflicting pieces of information, they disengage and choose to not believe the facts. For example, people underestimate the influence that conspiracy theories have on their own beliefs (Douglas & Sutton, 2008). Even fringe conspiracy theories that fail to convince people can nevertheless have negative effects such as reducing intent to reduce one's carbon footprint (Jolley & Douglas, 2014), decreasing trust in government (Einstein & Glick, 2014), and lowering support for climate action (van der Linden, 2015). The subversive nature of fake news was highlighted in a radio interview when Trump supporter and CNN political commentator Scottie Nell Hughes declared "there's no such thing, unfortunately, anymore [as] facts" (Rehm, 2016, par 45).

Different types of misinformation require different responses. Cook et al. (2017) found that informing people of the 97% consensus was effective in countering the negative influence of false-balance media coverage. However, explicit misinformation about the scientific consensus cancels out the positive effect of consensus information (van der Linden et al., 2017). This means that simply communicating the facts is insufficient to overcome explicit misinformation. As a consequence, inoculating interventions that explain the techniques used to distort facts are required to neutralize explicit misinformation.

Responding to climate misinformation

Given the dire impact of misinformation, how can we respond? Commonly, we look to undo the damage by refuting (or debunking) the misinformation. There exist a number of reviews of psychological research into debunking

(Lewandowsky et al., 2012; Swire & Ecker, 2018), with a concise set of guidelines summarized in Cook and Lewandowsky (2011).

A refutation of misinformation compels people to update their mental model of how the world works, removing the false piece of information. This creates a gap in their mental model and if the gap is left unfilled, the misinformation continues to influence (Seifert, 2002). However, people are less likely to rely on the misinformation if a factual alternative is supplied that fills the gap left by the vacated misinformation (Ecker, Lewandowsky, Cheung, & Maybery, 2015). The replacement fact should ideally be more plausible and easy-to-understand than the original misinformation (Baadte & Dutke, 2012). This dynamic is best summarized by the maxim: "fight sticky myths with stickier facts" (Heath & Heath, 2007).

The structure of a debunking determines its effectiveness. When debunking material places undue emphasis on the myth or introduces misinformation before flagging it as false, it increases the risk that the myth is mistakenly recalled as true (Peter & Koch, 2016; Skurnik, Yoon, Park, & Schwarz, 2005). There are several techniques that minimize this risk. First, providing a warning before mentioning the myth places people on cognitive alert and reduces their reliance on misinformation (Ecker, Lewandowsky, & Tang, 2010). Second, communicators should place more emphasis on the replacement fact designed to fill the gap left by the refuted misinformation.

While refuting misinformation is a necessary and often unavoidable activity, research points to a more optimal approach whenever available. Preemptively refuting misinformation before it is received (otherwise known as prebunking, Cook, 2016) is more effective at reducing the influence of misinformation than attempting to undo the damage after misinformation has been received (Bolsen & Druckman, 2015).

Prebunking is the new debunking

Inoculation theory offers a framework for effectively prebunking misinformation (McGuire & Papageorgis, 1961). This borrows the concept of inoculating against disease and applies it to knowledge, finding that exposing people to a "weak form of misinformation" is effective in helping people build immunity against the influence of misinformation. An inoculating text consists of two elements: a warning of the threat of being misinformed and counterarguments that refute the misinformation.

Inoculation has other benefits besides reducing the influence of misinformation. Ivanov et al. (2015) found that people exposed to an inoculating text were more likely to talk about the target issue. This indicates that inoculation carries the added bonus of helping break "climate silence", the phenomenon that people are reluctant to talk even with friends and family about climate change. Geiger and Swim (2016) found that even people who were concerned about climate change refrained from talking about the issue with their social networks.

Two studies into inoculating against climate misinformation have employed different forms of inoculation, offering a variety of approaches for communicators. Van der Linden et al. (2017) found that inoculations that refuted denialist arguments found in a specific piece of misinformation was effective in partially neutralizing the misinformation. Cook et al. (2017) found that explaining the techniques of misinformation in general terms, without specifically mentioning the misinformation, was effective in neutralizing a specific piece of misinformation. This indicates that it is possible to neutralize multiple instances of misinformation with a single inoculation framed in general terms.

Further, Cook et al. (2017) tested ways to inoculate against both implicit and explicit forms of misinformation. While inoculation text was useful against both forms of misinformation, communicating the 97% consensus was also effective against implicit misinformation. This has been replicated in another study that tested the influence of a John Oliver comedy video about false-balance media coverage of climate change (Brewer & McKnight, 2017). Watching the John Oliver video increased viewers' belief in global warming, as well as perceptions that most scientists believe in global warming. The video had the greatest effect on people with a low interest in climate.

These studies indicate that raising critical thinking skills is an effective way to build immunity to misinformation. One useful framework for explaining the argumentative techniques of misinformation are the five characteristics of science denial. These were first conceived by Hoofnagle (2007) and fleshed out further by Diethelm and McKee (2009). They are fake experts, logical fallacies, impossible expectations, cherry picking and conspiracy theories (summarized with the acronym FLICC, Cook et al., 2015).

Inoculating against misinformation by fostering critical thinking is an approach going back millennia. Aristotle argued that understanding the reasoning flaws of false arguments provided a more universal safeguard against faulty persuasion (Compton, 2005). Critical thinking is a powerful tool likened to "having x-ray vision into thinking" (van Gelder, 2005, p. 44). However, acquiring expertise in critical thinking is also difficult as it is a contrived, high-order skill requiring deliberate practice. Van Gelder equates mastering critical thinking to learning a second language. One way to facilitate this type of deeper learning is through educational programs.

Misconception-based learning

Misconception-based learning offers a practical and powerful way to inoculate people against misinformation (McCuin, Hayhoe, & Hayhoe, 2014). This is also known as agnotology-based learning (Bedford, 2010) or refutational teaching (Tippett, 2010). This teaching approach involves explicitly introducing misconceptions at the same time as communicating factual information.

Misconception-based learning has been shown to have a number of benefits relative to standard lessons that teach accurate information without mentioning misconceptions. A meta-analysis found that refutation text is the most useful form of educational text among elementary, high school and adult learners (Guzzetti, 2000). It has been shown to result in greater learning gains (McCuin et al., 2014; Muller, Bewes, Sharma, & Reimann, 2008) with longer effects than standard lessons (Guzzetti, 2000; McCuin et al., 2014). This teaching approach increases students' argumentative skills (Kuhn & Crowell, 2011) and fosters critical thinking skills (Berland & Reiser, 2008). Students also show more interest in refutational texts compared to traditional textbooks (Mason, Gava, & Boldrin, 2008).

Consequently, Frankie (2014) recommended that teachers would benefit from climate science courses that targeted climate change misconceptions. Further, Guzzo and Dall'Alba (2017) argued that educators should motivate their students to think critically, helping them to develop a better understanding of the world and be protected against misinformation. However, there is a current dearth of misconception-based learning material available to educators (Tippett 2010).

Nevertheless, misconception-based learning is being applied in various contexts. Bedford (2010) describes how a college class on climate change drew on misinformation texts to reinforce climate concepts taught earlier in the course. Cook, Bedford, and Mandia (2014) expand this work further, looking at efforts of misconception-based learning in educational and public communication contexts. Lambert and Bleicher (2017) instructed preservice teachers to research and rebut denialist claims and found that this was effective in increasing their understanding and perceptions about climate change. Lovitt and Shuyler (2016) had students evaluate the credibility and source of various climate science misconceptions and found students were able to distinguish between popular and scholarly literature, retaining their newly acquired information literacy skills after a four-week delay. Some teachers have re-purposed "teach the controversy" frames as a way to neutralize the controversy and introduced climate change topics in the classroom where it might not otherwise be included (Colston & Vadjunec, 2015). An online course, Making Sense of Climate Science Denial, adopted the approach of misconception-based learning, reaching over 26,000 students from 166 countries and providing video resources for teachers who enrolled in the course (Cook et al., 2015).

Educational efforts afford arguably the greatest opportunity to produce deeper, long-lasting reductions in the spread and influence of misinformation. However, short-term communication efforts are also required, when newly generated misinformation disseminated to the public requires an immediate response.

Fact checking and "technocognition"

Fact-checking is a necessary tool in countering and neutralizing misinformation. When political elites are made aware of the political consequences they might face from fact-checking, they become less likely to make false statements (Nyhan & Reifler, 2013). This is significant given the important role that political elites have on public opinions about climate change.

However, there are limitations to fact-checking. The quip, "a lie will go round the world while truth is pulling its boots on", underscores the unequal playing field between facts and misinformation. Accurately researching and publishing fact-based responses takes time, during which misinformation can disseminate quickly and influence a large number of people. Fact-checking, even if deployed successfully can also have minimal impact in some contexts. Swire, Berinsky, Lewandowsky, and Ecker (2017) found that even when Trump supporters read and accepted a refutation of a Trump statement, their intention to vote for him was unchanged.

Fact-checkers can also have unintended counterproductive effects. Levin (2017) found that when Facebook labelled a specific article as possible "fake news", it led to a number of conservative groups sharing the article, causing a surge in traffic. Similarly, an analysis of Facebook activity found that conspiratorial users increased their engagement with conspiracy posts after interacting with debunking posts (Zollo et al., 2017).

One way to maximize the effectiveness of fact-checking, while avoiding counterproductive outcomes, is a multi-disciplinary approach described as "technocognition" (Lewandowsky, Ecker, & Cook, 2017). This involves applying the insights of cognitive science in technological solutions. For example, online fact-checkers should adopt the recommendations of psychological research into debunking in order to minimize the risk of potential backfire effects where the debunking reinforces rather than reduces misperceptions.

Automatic detection of new misinformation is an emerging technology that can greatly enhance the effectiveness of online fact-checking efforts. Developing an automatic platform that can detect and assess the accuracy of new information is thought of as the "Holy Grail" of fact-checking (Hassan et al., 2015). Such a platform would need to monitor online information sources, spot claims, assess their reliability, and publish responses (Babaker & Moy, 2016).

Some automatic fact-checking solutions already exist. One Chrome browser extension tags the veracity of Facebook links based on the source's credibility and consistency with other news stories (Itkowitz, 2016). Using a knowledge representation derived from Wikipedia, Ciampaglia et al. (2015) was able to reliably assess truth value to statements. Ott, Choi, Cardie, and Hancock (2011) found that a combination of text categorization, classifiers and psycho-linguistic deception allowed them to detect deceptive text more accurately than most human judges.

While delivering fact-checking content is a necessary service, users are also encouraged to develop their own fact-checking, critical thinking skills. FactCheck.org published a set of practical steps to encourage closer reading and critical thinking (Kiely & Robertson, 2016), adopting key strategies such as checking sources, authors and consulting experts. Walton and Hepworth (2011) found that teaching information literacy through online social network learning was successful in conveying the ability to evaluate source material. Developing information literacy and critical thinking is consistent with the goals of misconception-based learning.

Conclusion

Misinformation is a serious societal issue that has become especially prevalent in recent years, as fake news has achieved mainstream attention. However, this is not a new phenomenon, particular in the area of climate change, and a large body of research can help us understand the structure and impact of misinformation. A key finding is that misinformation can cancel out the effect of accurate information, a result that has significant communication implications. It means that communicating the science is necessary but insufficient for communicators and educators looking to increase public levels of climate literacy. Further, the psychological research into debunking finds that undoing the impact of misinformation is difficult, and poorly designed attempts to debunk misinformation can be ineffective or counterproductive. Therefore, adopting an evidence-based communication approach that adopts the best-practices recommended by psychological research is essential.

To insulate our science communication efforts from misinformation, we need to accompany our science messages or lessons with inoculating text that explain the techniques used to distort the science. Inoculating text equips people with the critical thinking tools required to discern the truth when presented with conflicting pieces of information. Indeed, educational research has found that misconception-based learning is one of the most powerful and engaging ways to teach science. Not only does it more effectively increase science literacy levels, but it also increases critical thinking skills that neutralize the influence of misinformation. Consequently, our current predicament of fake news, while dire, also presents opportunities for communicators and educators. Misconception-based learning, if deployed widely enough in classrooms, could potentially eradicate climate science denial in the same way that vaccination eradicated polio.

References

Akter, S., Bennett, J., & Ward, M.B. (2012). Climate change scepticism and public support for mitigation: Evidence from an Australian choice experiment. *Global Environmental Change, 22*(3): 736 - 745. DOI: 10.1016/j.gloenvcha.2012.05.004.

Anderegg, W. R. L., Prall, J. W., Harold, J., & Schneider, S. H. (2010). Expert credibility in climate change. *Proceedings of the National Academy of Sciences of the United States of America, 107,* 12107-12109.

Baadte, C., & Dutke, S. (2012). Learning about persons: the effects of text structure and executive capacity on conceptual change. *European Journal of Psychology of Education, 28,* 1045–1064. http://doi.org/10.1007/s10212-012-0153-2

Babaker, M., & Moy, W. (2016). The state of automated fact checking. *Full-Fact.org.* Retrieved from https://fullfact.org/media/uploads/full_fact-the_state_of_automated_factchecking_aug_2016.pdf

Bedford, D. (2010). Agnotology as a teaching tool: Learning climate science by studying misinformation. *Journal of Geography, 109*(4), 159-165. https://doi.org/10.1080/00221341.2010.498121

Berland, L. K., & Reiser, B. J. (2009). Making sense of argumentation and explanation. *Science Education, 93*(1), 26-55. https://doi.org/10.1002/sce.20286

Bessi, A. and Ferrara, E. (2016, November 7). Social bots distort the 2016 US presidential election online discussion. *First Monday, 21*(11 – 7). Retrieved from https://ssrn.com/abstract=2982233

Bolsen, T., & Druckman, J. N. (2015). Counteracting the politicization of science. *Journal of Communication, 65*(5), 745-769. https://doi.org/10.1111/jcom.12171

Boussalis, C., & Coan, T. G. (2016). Text-mining the signals of climate change doubt. *Global Environmental Change, 36,* 89-100. DOI: 10.1016/j.gloenvcha.2015.12.001.

Brewer, P. R., & McKnight, J. (2017). A statistically representative climate change debate: Satirical television news, scientific consensus, and public perceptions of global warming. *Atlantic Journal of Communication, 25*(3), 166-180. https://doi.org/10.1080/15456870.2017.1324453

Brulle, R. J. (2014). Institutionalizing delay: foundation funding and the creation of US climate change counter-movement organizations. *Climatic Change, 122*(4), 681-694. DOI: 10.1007/s10584-013-1018-7

Campbell, T. H., & Kay, A. C. (2014). Solution aversion: On the relation between ideology and motivated disbelief. *Journal of Personality and Social Psychology, 107*(5), 809. DOI: 10.1037/a0037963

Capstick, S. B., & Pidgeon, N. F. (2014). What is climate change scepticism? Examination of the concept using a mixed methods study of the UK public. *Global Environmental Change, 24*, 389-401. https://doi.org/10.1016/j.gloenvcha.2013.08.012

Carlton, J. S., Perry-Hill, R., Huber, M., & Prokopy, L. S. (2015). The climate change consensus extends beyond climate scientists. *Environmental Research Letters, 10*(9), 094025.

Carmichael, J. T., & Brulle, R. J. (2017). Elite cues, media coverage, and public concern: an integrated path analysis of public opinion on climate change, 2001–2013. *Environmental Politics, 26*(2), 232-252.

Chang, C. H., & Pascua, L. (2015). 'The hole in the sky causes global warming': A case study of secondary school students' climate change alternative conceptions. *Review of International Geographical Education Online (RIGEO), 5*(3), 316.

Ciampaglia, G. L., Shiralkar, P., Rocha, L. M., Bollen, J., Menczer, F., & Flammini, A. (2015). Computational fact checking from knowledge networks. *PLoS ONE, 10*, 1-13. doi: 10.1371/journal.pone.0128193

Colston, N. M., & Vadjunec, J. M. (2015). A critical political ecology of consensus: On "Teaching Both Sides" of climate change controversies. *Geoforum, 65*, 255-265. https://doi.org/10.1016/j.geoforum.2015.08.006

Compton, J. (2005). Comparison, contrast, and synthesis of Aristotelian rationality and inoculation. *Journal of the Speech and Theatre Association of Missouri, 35*, 1-23.

Cook, J. (2016). Countering climate science denial and communicating scientific consensus. *Oxford Encyclopedia of Climate Change Communication.* London: Oxford University Press.

Cook, J., Bedford, D. & Mandia, S. (2014). Raising climate literacy through addressing misinformation: Case studies in agnotology-based learning. *Journal of Geoscience Education, 62*(3), 296-306. https://doi.org/10.5408/13-071.1

Cook, J., & Lewandowsky, S. (2011). *The debunking handbook.* St. Lucia, Australia: University of Queensland.

Cook, J., Lewandowsky, S., & Ecker, U. (2017). Neutralizing misinformation through inoculation: Exposing misleading argumentation techniques reduces their influence. *PLOS ONE, 12*(5): e0175799. https://doi.org/10.1371/journal.pone.0175799

Cook, J., Nuccitelli, D., Green, S.A., Richardson, M., Winkler, B., Painting, R., Way, R., Jacobs, P., & Skuce, A. (2013). Quantifying the consensus on anthropogenic global warming in the scientific literature. *Environmental Research Letters, 8*(2), 024024, 1-7.

Cook, J., Oreskes, N., Doran, P. T., Anderegg, W. R., Verheggen, B., Maibach, E. W., Carlton, J. S., Lewandowsky, S., Skuce, A. G., Green, S. A., & Nuccitelli, D. (2016). Consensus on consensus: a synthesis of consensus estimates on human-caused global warming. *Environmental Research Letters, 11*(4), 048002.

Cook, J., Schuennemann, K., Nuccitelli, D., Jacobs, P., Cowtan, K., Green, S., Way, R., Richardson, M., Cawley, G., Mandia, S., Skuce, A., & Bedford, D. (2015, April). Denial101x: Making Sense of Climate Science Denial. *edX.* Retrieved from http://edx.org/understanding-climate-denial

Davidson, E., & McNutt, M. K. (2017, August 2). Red/blue and peer review. *Eos, 98.* https://doi.org/10.1029/2017EO078943

De Pryck, K., & Gemenne, F. (2017). The denier-in-chief: Climate change, science and the election of Donald J. Trump. *Law and Critique, 28*(2), 119-126.

Diethelm, P., & McKee, M. (2009). Denialism: what is it and how should scientists respond? *The European Journal of Public Health, 19*(1), 2-4. doi:10.1093/eurpub/ckn139

Ding, D., Maibach, E. W., Zhao, X., Roser-Renouf, C., & Leiserowitz, A. (2011). Support for climate policy and societal action are linked to perceptions about scientific agreement. *Nature Climate Change, 1*(9), 462.

Doran, P. T., & Zimmerman, M. K. (2009). Examining the scientific consensus on climate change. *Eos, Transactions American Geophysical Union, 90*(3), 22-23.

Douglas, K. M., & Sutton, R. M. (2008). The hidden impact of conspiracy theories: Perceived and actual influence of theories surrounding the death of Princess Diana. *The Journal of Social Psychology, 148*(2), 210-222. https://doi.org/10.3200/SOCP.148.2.210-222.

Ecker, U. K. H., Lewandowsky, S., Cheung, C. S. C., & Maybery, M. T. (2015). He did it! She did it! No, she did not! Multiple causal explanations and the continued influence of misinformation. *Journal of Memory and Language, 85,*101–115.

Ecker, U.K.H., Lewandowsky, S., & Tang, D.T.W. (2010). Explicit warnings reduce but do not eliminate the continued influence of misinformation. *Memory & Cognition, 38,* 1087–1100. DOI: 10.3758/MC.38.8.1087

Einstein, K. L., & Glick, D. M. (2014). Do I think BLS data are BS? The consequences of conspiracy theories. *Political Behavior, 37*(3), 679-701. doi:10.1007/s11109-014-9287-z

Farrell, J. (2016). Network structure and influence of the climate change counter-movement. *Nature Climate Change, 6*(4), 370-374.

Flood, A. (2016). 'Post-truth' named word of the year by Oxford Dictionaries. *The Guardian.* Retrieved from https://www.theguardian.com/books/2016/nov/15/post-truth-named-word-of-the-year-by-oxford-dictionaries

Frankie, Thomas J. (2014). *Facing the controversy: A grounded theory study of how teachers plan to address climate change in their class rooms* (Doctoral dissertation). Retrieved from https://fisherpub.sjfc.edu/cgi/viewcontent.cgi?referer=https://www.google.com/&httpsredir=1&article=1192&context=education_etd

Gautier, C., Deutsch, K., & Rebich, S. (2006). Misconceptions about the greenhouse effect. *Journal of Geoscience Education, 54*(3), 386.

Geiger, N., & Swim, J. K. (2016). Climate of silence: Pluralistic ignorance as a barrier to climate change discussion. *Journal of Environmental Psychology, 47*, 79-90. https://doi.org/10.1016/j.jenvp.2016.05.002

Glaeser, E. L., Ponzetto, G. A., & Shapiro, J. M. (2005). Strategic extremism: Why Republicans and Democrats divide on religious values. *The Quarterly Journal of Economics, 120*(4), 1283-1330.

Guzzetti, B. J. (2000). Learning counter-intuitive science concepts: What have we learned from over a decade of research? *Reading & Writing Quarterly, 16*, 89–98. https://doi.org/10.1080/105735600277971

Guzzo, G. B., & Dall'Alba, G. (2017). What is an ideal critical thinker expected to conclude about anthropogenic global warming? *Philosophical Inquiry in Education, 24*(3), 223-236.

Hassan, N., Adair, B., Hamilton, J., Li, C., Tremayne, M., Yang, J., & Yu, C. (2015). *The Quest to Automate Fact-Checking.* Proceedings of the 2015 Computation + Journalism Symposium.

Heath, C., & Heath, D. (2007). *Made to stick: Why some ideas survive and others die.* New York: Random House.

Hoofnagle, M. (2007, April 30). Hello Scienceblogs. Denialism Blog. Retrieved from http://scienceblogs.com/denialism/about/

Hornsey, M. J., Harris, E. A., Bain, P. G., & Fielding, K. S. (2016). Meta-analyses of the determinants and outcomes of belief in climate change. *Nature Climate Change, 6*(6), 622-626.

Itkowitz, C. (2016, Nov 20). Fake news is a real problem. These college students came up with a fix. *Washington Post.* Retrieved from http://www.chicagotribune.com/bluesky/technology/ct-fake-news-college-students-fix-wp-bsi-20161120-story.html

Ivanov, B., Sims, J. D., Compton, J., Miller, C. H., Parker, K. A., Parker, J. L., Harrison, K., & Averbeck, J. M. (2015). The general content of postinoculation talk: Recalled issue-specific conversations following inoculation treatments. *Western Journal of Communication, 79*(2), 218-238. https://doi.org/10.1080/10570314.2014.943423

Jacques, P. J., Dunlap, R. E., & Freeman, M. (2008). The organisation of denial: Conservative think tanks and environmental scepticism. *Environmental Politics, 17*(3), 349-385. https://doi.org/10.1080/09644010802055576

Jasny, L., Waggle, J., & Fisher, D. R. (2015). An empirical examination of echo chambers in US climate policy networks. *Nature Climate Change, 5*(8), 782-786. DOI: 10.1038/nclimate2666

Joireman, J., Truelove, H. B., & Duell, B. (2010). Effect of outdoor temperature, heat primes and anchoring on belief in global warming. *Journal of Environmental Psychology, 30*(4), 358-367. http://dx.doi.org/10.1016/j.jenvp.2010.03.004

Jolley, D., & Douglas, K. M. (2014). The social consequences of conspiracism: Exposure to conspiracy theories decreases intentions to engage in politics and to reduce one's carbon footprint. *British Journal of Psychology, 105*(1), 35-56. https://doi.org/10.1111/bjop.12018

Kiely, E., & Robertson, L. (2016). How to Spot Fake News. *FactCheck.org.* Retrieved from http://www.factcheck.org/2016/11/how-to-spot-fake-news/

Kollanyi, B., Howard, P. N., & Woolley, S. C. (2016). Bots and automation over Twitter during the first U.S. presidential debate. *Comprop Data Memo.* Retrieved from https://assets.documentcloud.org/documents/3144967/Trump-Clinton-Bots-Data.pdf

Kollipara, P. (2015, January 21). Wrap-up: U.S. Senate agrees climate change is real—but not necessarily that humans are causing it. *Science.* Retrieved from http://www.sciencemag.org/news/2015/01/wrap-us-senate-agrees-climate-change-real-not-necessarily-humans-are-causing-it

Kuhn, D., & Crowell, A. (2011). Dialogic argumentation as a vehicle for developing young adolescents' thinking. *Psychological Science, 22*(4), 545-552. https://doi.org/10.1177/0956797611402512

Kuklinski, J. H., Quirk, P. J., Jerit, J., Schwieder, D., & Rich, R. F. (2000). Misinformation and the currency of democratic citizenship. *The Journal of Politics, 62*(3), 790-816.

Lambert, J. L., & Bleicher, R. E. (2017). Argumentation as a strategy for increasing preservice teachers' understanding of climate change, a key global socioscientific issue. *International Journal of Education in Mathematics, Science and Technology, 5*(1), 101-112.

Leiserowitz, A., Smith, N., & Marlon, J. R. (2011). American teens' knowledge of climate change (Report No. 5). New Haven, CT: Yale Project on Climate Change Communication.

Leiserowitz, A., Maibach, E., Roser-Renouf, C., Rosenthal, S., & Cutler, M. (2017). Climate change in the American mind: May 2017. New Haven, CT: Yale Program on Climate Change Communication. Retrieved from http://climatecommunication.yale.edu/wp-content/uploads/2017/07/Climate-Change-American-Mind-May-2017.pdf

Levin, S. (2017, May 16). Facebook promised to tackle fake news. But the evidence shows it's not working. *The Guardian.* Retrieved from https://www.theguardian.com/technology/2017/may/16/facebook-fake-news-tools-not-working

Leviston, Z., Walker, I., & Morwinski, S. (2013). Your opinion on climate change might not be as common as you think. *Nature Climate Change, 3*(4), 334.

Lewandowsky, S., Ecker, U. K. H., & Cook, J. (2017). Beyond misinformation: understanding and coping with the post-truth era. *Journal of Applied Research in Memory and Cognition, 6*(4), 353-369. https://doi.org/10.1016/j.jarmac.2017.07.008

Lewandowsky, S., Ecker, U. K., Seifert, C. M., Schwarz, N., & Cook, J. (2012). Misinformation and its correction continued influence and successful debiasing. *Psychological Science in the Public Interest, 13*(3), 106-131.

Li, Y., Johnson, E. J., & Zaval, L. (2011). Local Warming: Daily Temperature Change Influences Belief in Global Warming. *Psychological Science, 22*(4), 454–459. https://doi.org/10.1177/0956797611400913

Lovitt, C. F., & Shuyler, K. (2016). Teaching climate change concepts and the nature of science: A library activity to identify sources of climate change misconceptions. In *Integrating Information Literacy into the Chemistry Curriculum* (pp. 221-246). American Chemical Society.

Mason, L., Gava, M., & Boldrin, A. (2008). On warm conceptual change: The interplay of text, epistemological beliefs, and topic interest. *Journal of Educational Psychology, 100*(2), 291. DOI: 10.1037/0022-0663.100.2.291

Matthews, D. (2017). Donald Trump has tweeted climate change skepticism 115 times. Here's all of it. *Vox.* Retrieved from https://www.vox.com/policy-and-politics/2017/6/1/15726472/trump-tweets-global-warming-paris-climate-agreement

Mazo, J. (2013). Climate change: strategies of denial. *Survival, 55*(4), 41-49. https://doi.org/10.1080/00396338.2013.823019

McCright, A. M., Charters, M., Dentzman, K., & Dietz, T. (2016). Examining the effectiveness of climate change frames in the face of a climate denial counter-frame. *Topics in Cognitive Science, 8*(1), 76-97. https://doi.org/10.1111/tops.12171

McCright, A. M., & Dunlap, R. E. (2000). Challenging global warming as a social problem: An analysis of the conservative movement's counter-claims. *Social Problems, 47*(4), 499-522.

McCuin, J. L., Hayhoe, K., & Hayhoe, D. (2014). Comparing the effects of traditional vs. misconceptions-based instruction on student understanding of the greenhouse effect. *Journal of Geoscience Education, 62*(3), 445-459. https://doi.org/10.5408/13-068.1

McGuire, W. J., & Papageorgis, D. (1961). The relative efficacy of various types of prior belief-defense in producing immunity against persuasion. *Public Opinion Quarterly, 26*, 24-34. http://dx.doi.org/10.1037/h0042026

Mildenberger, M., & Leiserowitz, A. (2017). Public opinion on climate change: Is there an economy–environment tradeoff? *Environmental Politics, 26(5)*, 801-824. https://doi.org/10.1080/09644016.2017.1322275

Muller, D. A., Bewes, J., Sharma, M. D., & Reimann, P. (2008). Saying the wrong thing: Improving learning with multimedia by including misconceptions. *Journal of Computer Assisted Learning, 24*(2), 144-155. DOI: 10.1111/j.1365-2729.2007.00248.x

Nerlich, B. (2010). "Climategate": Paradoxical metaphors and political paralysis. *Environmental Values, 19*, 419-442. DOI: 10.2307/25764266.

New York Times (2016). Donald Trump's New York Times interview: Full transcript. Retrieved from https://www.nytimes.com/2016/11/23/us/politics/trump-new-york-times-interview-transcript.html

Nyhan, B., & Reifler, J. (2015). The effect of fact-checking on elites: A field experiment on US State legislators. *American Journal of Political Science, 59*(3), 628-640. https://doi.org/10.1111/ajps.12162

Ott, M., Choi, Y., Cardie, C., & Hancock, J. T. (2011, June). Finding deceptive opinion spam by any stretch of the imagination. *In Proceedings of the 49th Annual Meeting of the Association for Computational Linguistics: Human*

Language Technologies-Volume 1 (pp. 309-319). Association for Computational Linguistics.

Painter, J., & Ashe, T. (2012). Cross-national comparison of the presence of climate scepticism in the print media in six countries, 2007–10. *Environmental Research Letters, 7*(4), 044005.

Peter, C., & Koch, T. (2016). When debunking scientific myths fails (and when it does not): The backfire effect in the context of journalistic coverage and immediate judgments as prevention strategy. *Science Communication, 38,* 3–25. https://doi.org/10.1177/1075547015613523

Peterson, C. (1989, May 9). Experts, OMB spar on global warming: "Greenhouse Effect" may be accelerating, scientists tell hearing. *Washington Post.* Retrieved from https://www.washingtonpost.com/archive/politics/1989/05/09/experts-omb-spar-on-global-warming/7fc219d4-4693-4663-bf83-319fa97d7dda/

Politifact (2017). Donald Trump's file. *Politifact.* Retrieved from http://www.politifact.com/personalities/donald-trump/

Poortinga, W., Spence, A., Whitmarsh, L., Capstick, S., & Pidgeon, N. F. (2011). Uncertain climate: An investigation into public scepticism about anthropogenic climate change. *Global Environmental Change, 21*(3), 1015-1024.

Qiu, X., Oliveira, D., Shirazi, A.S. Flammini, A. & Menczer F. (2017). Limited individual attention and online virality of low-quality information. *Nature Human Behaviour. 1*(7):0132. Doi: 10.1038/s41562-017-0132

Rahmstorf, S. (2004). The climate sceptics. *Perspektiven, 3,* 76-83. Retrieved from http://www.pik-potsdam.de/~stefan/Publications/Other/rahmstorf_climate_sceptics_2004.pdf

Ranney, M.A. & Clark, D. (2016). Climate change conceptual change: Scientific information can transform attitudes. *Topics in Cognitive Science, 8*(1), 49-75. https://doi.org/10.1111/tops.12187

Readfearn, G. (2016). Revealed: Most popular climate story on social media told half a million people the science was a hoax. *Desmogblog.* Retrieved from https://www.desmogblog.com/2016/11/29/revealed-most-popular-climate-story-social-media-told-half-million-people-science-was-hoax

Rehm, D. (2016, November 30). How journalists are rethinking their role under a Trump Presidency. Retrieved from http://dianerehm.org/shows/2016-11-30/how-journalists-are-rethinking-their-role-under-a-trump-presidency

Seifert, C. M. (2002). The continued influence of misinformation in memory: What makes a correction effective? *The Psychology of Learning and Motivation, 41,* 265–292.

Skurnik, I., Yoon, C., Park, D.C., & Schwarz, N. (2005). How warnings about false claims become recommendations. *Journal of Consumer Research, 31,* 713–724. DOI: 10.1086/426605

Swire, B., Berinsky, A. J., Lewandowsky, S., & Ecker, U. K. (2017). Processing political misinformation: comprehending the Trump phenomenon. *Royal Society Open Science, 4*(3), 160802. https://doi.org/10.1098/rsos.160802

Swire, B. & Ecker, U. K. H. (2018). Misinformation and its correction: Cognitive mechanisms and recommendations for mass communication. In. B. Southwell, E. A. Thorson, & L. Sheble. (Eds), *Misinformation and Mass Audiences*. Austin, TX: University of Texas Press.

Thompson, J. E. (2017). Survey data reflecting popular opinions of the causes and mitigation of climate change. *Data in Brief.* http://dx.doi.org/10.1016/j.dib.2017.07.060

Tippett, C. D. (2010). Refutation text in science education: A review of two decades of research. *International Journal of Science and Mathematics Education, 8*(6), 951-970. DOI: 10.1007/s10763-010-9203-x

Trump, D. [realDonaldTrump] (2012a, June 29). Interesting -- studies show that wind farms have a warming effect on the climate [tweet]. Retrieved from https://twitter.com/realDonaldTrump/status/218790317242068993

Trump, D. [realDonaldTrump] (2012b, November 6). The concept of global warming was created by and for the Chinese in order to make U.S. manufacturing non-competitive [tweet]. Retrieved from https://twitter.com/realdonaldtrump/status/265895292191248385

Trump, D. [realDonaldTrump] (2013a, June 26). Obama's speech on climate change was scary. It will lower our standard of living and raise costs of fuel & food for everyone. [tweet]. Retrieved from https://twitter.com/realDonaldTrump/status/349973299889057792

Trump, D. [realDonaldTrump] (2013b, November 23). They changed the name global warming to climate change because the concept of global warming just wasn't working! [tweet]. Retrieved from https://twitter.com/realDonaldTrump/status/404420095113715712

Trump, D. [realDonaldTrump] (2014a, February 18). "@Michael_KSC: @realDonaldTrump @thedropkicks Whether Global Warming or Climate change. The fact is We didn't cause it. We cannot change it. [tweet]. Retrieved from https://twitter.com/realDonaldTrump/status/435741126440808448

Trump, D. [realDonaldTrump] (2014b, October 29). Just out - the POLAR ICE CAPS are at an all time high, the POLAR BEAR population has never been stronger. Where the hell is global warming? [tweet]. Retrieved from https://twitter.com/realDonaldTrump/status/527388136306143232

van der Linden, S. (2015). The conspiracy-effect: Exposure to conspiracy theories (about global warming) decreases pro-social behavior and science acceptance. *Personality and Individual Differences, 87*, 171-173. https://doi.org/10.1016/j.paid.2015.07.045

van der Linden, S., Leiserowitz, A., Rosenthal, S., & Maibach, E. (2017). Inoculating the public against misinformation about climate change. *Global Challenges, 1*(2), 1600008, 1-7. https://doi.org/10.1002/gch2.201600008

van Gelder, T. (2005). Teaching critical thinking: Some lessons from cognitive science. *College Teaching, 53*(1), 41-48.

Walton, G., & Hepworth, M. (2011). A longitudinal study of changes in learners' cognitive states during and following an information literacy teaching intervention. *Journal of Documentation, 67*(3), 449-479. DOI: 10.1108/00220411111124541

Washington Post (2017). 100 days of Trump claims. *Washington Post*. Retrieved from https://www.washingtonpost.com/graphics/politics/trump-claims/

Weng, L., Flammini, A., Vespignani, A., & Menczer, F. (2012). Competition among memes in a world with limited attention. *Scientific Reports, 2*, 335.

World Economic Forum (2014). Outlook on the Global Agenda 2014. *World Economic Forum*. http://reports.weforum.org/outlook-14/view/top-ten-trends-category-page/10-the-rapid-spread-of-misinformation-online/

Woods, R., Fernandez, A., & Coen, S. (2010). The use of religious metaphors by UK newspapers to describe and denigrate climate change. *Public Understanding of Science, 20*(10), 1-17.

Zollo, F., Bessi, A., Del Vicario, M., Scala, A., Caldarelli, G., Shekhtman, L., Havlin, S. & Quattrociocchi, W. (2017). Debunking in a world of tribes. *arXiv preprint*. arXiv:1510.04267. https://doi.org/10.1371/journal.pone.0181821

Chapter 3

Intentional Circumvention: Navigating Around Denial and Towards Each Other

Anthony Rogers-Wright

Introduction

Climate denial is nothing new. One of the industries most responsible for greenhouse gas emissions knew their products were causing damage to the atmosphere since the 1970s, and was exposed by the investigative reporting of the *Los Angeles Times* and *Inside Climate News* (Banerjee, Song, & Hasemyer, 2015). Exxon, "*without revealing all that it had learned, worked at the forefront of climate denial, manufacturing doubt about the scientific consensus that its own scientists had confirmed*" (Banerjee et al., 2015, para. 2).

The praxis of climate denial involves the expenditure of tens of millions of dollars on think tanks, white papers, and investments in the form of campaign contributions to candidates and lawmakers who continue to question and/or deny the science Exxon itself knew to be accurate for nearly 40 years (Banerjee et al., 2015). Donald Trump is not the first president to write off, if not, assault climate science. His GOP predecessor, George W. Bush, and henchmen, Dick Cheney and Karl Rove, initiated a program of denial almost immediately after taking office. As reported by Rolling Stone Magazine in 2007, "*in a fax sent to the CEQ on February 6th, 2001—two weeks after Bush took office—ExxonMobil's top lobbyist, Randy Randol, demanded a housecleaning of the scientists in charge of studying global warming*" (Dickinson, 2007, para. 13).

The age of Trumpism is not much different from that of George W. Bush, except for the increased urgency at a time when scientists have revealed even more dire consequences associated with climate change. They have instructed us to leave 80 percent of remaining fossil fuels in the ground (Hayes, 2014; Carrington, 2015), a prospect that would cost the industry of Trump's previous Secretary of State trillions of dollars in revenue (Rex Tillerson was the CEO of ExxonMobil until joining the Trump administration). But as author Naomi Klein writes in her latest book, *No is Not Enough: Resisting Trump's Shock Politics and Winning The World We Need*, "*Trump, as extreme as he is, is less an aberration than a logical conclusion – a pastiche of pretty much all the worst trends of the past half century*" (Klein, 2017, P.9). Essentially, our communication medium as social/climate justice practitioners cannot operate from a platform of "*Trump Shock*", for reasons discussed later in this chapter.

Our communication should be informed by the fact that portraying climate change in a way that shifts from concept to mobilization is a byzantine exercise, even without climate denial and the think tanks that fuel it. Author Rob Nixon in his book, *Slow Violence and the Environmentalism of the Poor* (2013), describes climate change itself as not portrayed in a way that invites people to view it as a form of violence. Nixon states, "*By slow violence I mean a violence that occurs gradually occurs and out of sight, a violence of delayed destruction that is dispersed across time and space, an attritional violence that is typically not viewed as violence at all*" (2013, p. 2). In proposing a solution, Nixon goes on to say that we need to:

> *Engage a different kind of violence, a violence that is neither spectacular nor instantaneous, but rather incremental and accretive, its calamitous repercussions playing out across a range of temporal scales … we also need to engage the representational, narrative and strategic challenges posed by the relative invisibility of slow violence.* (2013, p.2)

To understand how climate change denial gained traction, it could be useful to contrast climate denial with other fringe conspiracy theories such as Holocaust denial. As troubling as it is that there exists a community of Holocaust denialists, they are rightfully treated as fringe and summarily dismissed. I believe, in addition to the undeniable documentation available for all to see, it's the powerful and profound stories told by Holocaust survivors like Viktor Frankl, and others like Steven Spielberg, that render Holocaust denial as quixotic and frivolous. These stories have also served as key reminders of the continued challenge and dangers of anti-Semitism and all forms of bigotry. Despite the narrative challenges in telling climate stories, it is through storytelling that we can likewise move communities to action and heightened vigilance.

Addressing the representational and narrative challenges of the climate crisis are key to moving forward in the age of Trump and beyond. We must ask ourselves not just *what* we are communicating, but *how* we are communicating. This is where storytelling becomes increasingly imperative.

As it pertains to representation, the majority of the U.S. "Left" and its non-profit apparatus have historically performed poorly in representing the disproportionate impacts of the climate crisis on marginalized communities, specifically low-wealth communities and communities of color, and even more specifically, Native American communities. The everyday struggles of, and impacts experienced by, these communities, are too seldom transmitted by those in the environmental "movement" with the biggest transistors and budgets, who have demonstrated more of an affinity to discuss individual "climate exacerbated" storms themselves, a selected piece of fossil fuel infrastructure, and the preservation of wildlife, especially, the unofficial logo of the climate community, the polar bear.

Communicating climate change in a way that increases mobilization should take examples of the stories offered to us by Holocaust survivors and render them into a model. Storytelling is not only a way to address the climate crisis—it also serves as a key component of our lifeblood in a way that compels us to portray the stories and experiences of people most impacted by the climate crisis as well as the myriad forms of injustice that contribute to it. But in evaluating how we communicate, we must also consider our messaging, which too frequently operates from a standpoint of *No*—no more fossil fuels, no more carbon pollution, etc. As Klein reminds us, we must get to the "*Yes*" in our communications and operations.

Getting to the *Yes* in our storytelling, increasing representation and altering our entire narrative requires a practice known as *Back Casting*, "*a method in which the future desired conditions are envisioned and steps are then defined to attain those conditions, rather than taking steps that are merely a continuation of present methods extrapolated into the future*" (Holmberg & Robert, 2000, p. 294). What follows below is a discussion of what we can't do, the challenges of confronting a culture of climate denial through communication, and the ways in which stories can overcome these challenges while also mobilizing more people into the climate fight.

Beyond force against force

When Morhei Uyeshiba developed Aikido, his primary goal was not to defeat opponents. The idea, as Uyeshiba saw it, was to remove aggression from the opponent's intent and yield to their force such that the opponent's own aggressiveness leads to their own demise. Rather than meet the opponent with similar or overpowering force, Akido instructs students to move out of the lane of attack, using the opponent's own momentum to vanquish them. Essentially, rather than attempting to block or oppose a strike, the Aikido pedagogy involves shepherding the opponent's power by determining the direction of an attack to first avoid it and then utilize it ("Aikido, Judo, Jujitsu and Karate - Comparing Different Martial Arts," 2008).

Climate scientists and climate justice advocates would do well to embrace the paradigm of Aikido. In many ways, we have no other choice if part of our goal is to effect change in the attitudes and behaviors of so-called climate deniers. And it's not just the fact that right-wing think tanks have outmaneuvered their liberal counterparts with focused and intentional financial investment, nor the previous and current electoral successes of the conservative wings of both major political parties. The largest obstacle, as discussed in INCITE!'s seminal work, *The Revolution Will Not Be Funded: Beyond The Non Profit Industrial Complex* (2017), is the fact that, "the well-heeled and strategic philanthropy of conservative foundations have successfully moved national ideology, and hence, policy towards the right." INCITE also cites the work of Sally Covington who, in a 1997 report for the National Committee for Responsive Philanthropy, analyzed the giving patterns of 12 prominent conservative foundations. Covington stated, "These 12 funders directed a majority of their grants to organizations and programs that pursue an overtly ideological agenda based on industrial and environmental deregulation" (1997, p. 3).

The result is that these conservative foundations, and the think tanks they continue to fund, have shaped a national ideology. They have also established a robust national culture rooted in climate denial, climate skepticism, and a paradigm that equates addressing climate change with economic compression of the American standard of life. All without overtly acknowledging an economic engine driven largely by the extraction and emission of fossil fuels. In short, we have to be honest and admit the truth: they've told their story in a more effective way than the climate community, and have established a pernicious culture of climate denial in the process.

The culture of capitalism was not created overnight, over years, or even over decades. It's been in the making for generations: generations of wars, advertisements, racism, bigotry, heteropatriarchy and the communication medium that keeps these variables intact. And for reasons discussed by thinkers like Professor Andrew J. Hoffman in his book, *How Culture Shapes the Climate Change Debate* (2015), we cannot overcome this medium simply with better or more forceful communication. We must not employ a "force on force" praxis - to circumvent the communication of climate denial, we must first better comprehend the culture of climate denial.

The intransigence of culture

One phenomenon that has become more prevalent in the age of Trump is the debate over *"alternative facts"* and *"fake news."* Both sides of the political spectrum evoke these phrases when media produces reports and stories that abash or otherwise criticize their political candidate or issue of choice. Journalistic slants and proclamations are so obvious they have become superficial – it's gotten to the point where simply revealing which cable news channel one watches the most immediately reveals political and social affiliations.

Even cable news channels reporting on the exact same topic will have different analyses, heroes and villains based on the network's political affiliation, and different conclusions of who is to laud and who is to blame. MSNBC reports that an unarmed African American was murdered by police; Fox News reports that the same African American, with a checkered past as proven by displaying select photographs, was uncooperative and ultimately killed because the officer feared for their life. As Rashad Robinson, director of the Black liberation organization, Color of Change, explains, "criminalization occurs when images chosen by media consciously or unconsciously create a justification for why people of color are killed" (Lewis, 2014, par 8).

But perhaps the biggest takeaway of what Robinson highlights, is that Fox and MSNBC are both keenly aware that culture determines not simply *how* information is processed, but also *if* it is even processed at all - a scenario that is adroitly documented by Professor Andrew J. Hoffman (2015). Hoffman documents how we employ ideological filters, influenced by belief systems, or "motivated reasoning," when analyzing facts and data. These filters are largely determined by the groups that we belong to, referred to as "cultural cognition" (2015, p. 4). Our group values, which greatly influence us, create a desire to remain consistent with the beliefs and values that we and those we trust and value most. Once these beliefs are established, Hoffman asserts that people develop "biased assimilation," giving greater weight to evidence and arguments that support our pre-existing values and beliefs and "disconfirmation bias" in which we expend even greater energy in refuting evidence and arguments that are not congruent with our values and beliefs (2015, p. 17).

One characterization of culture discusses the act of developing intellectual and moral faculties. The time it takes to develop these variables, in some cases our entire lives, renders facts into *alternate facts* and news into *fake news*. It's like watching a sporting event and observing how we react to a contested call made by an officiator. No matter what the instant replay shows us, if the call benefited the team we support it was a great call—if it disadvantages our team, we got screwed. And there are numerous reasons why our team got screwed, *the official was born near the city of the opposing team,* we might try and explain, or *the official was quoted as praising a player from the opposite team.* As Hoffman concludes, "As such we are less likely to debate a person's ideas and more likely to question their motives. We first try to determine if the person we engage with is part of our 'tribe' and therefore someone whose ideas we can trust" (2015, p. 17).

Climate denialists and their agents have a marked advantage in the monetary investments made in developing their culture. In 1995, conservative think tanks such as the Heritage Foundation, the American Enterprise Institute and the Cato Institute had a collective revenue base of over $77 million. Their liberal counterparts including the Center for Community Change the Twentieth Century Fund and the Institute for Policy Studies had less than $20 million (INCITE!, 2017). The denialists used their monetary advantage to better prove that they have the ideas that can be trusted – and in numerous ways, this tactic was efficacious.

Denialists also have the advantage in another form of currency that, like the petroleum products they lobby for, is not renewable—time. They have all the time in the world to maintain the status quo, whereas climate action advocates know time is running out to save lives and physical systems of the planet. The same amount of time that it has taken, roughly 40 years, to develop the culture of climate denial will lead to massive loss of life and the drawdown of numerous social systems if we continue a slash, burn, and emit economy. Culture is obstinate and intransigent, it won't change overnight, it may never change for that matter. And since we don't have the time to counter the culture of climate denial in a straight line, we will need to find shortcuts that are effective. We're going to have to circumvent it and we need to do so intentionally.

The gravity of climate denial

One of the common retorts of climate skeptics is, "the climate is always changing" (Cook, 2017 par 2). There is as much science that explains why fossil fuel emissions are having a nearly irreparable effect on the natural and social systems of our planet as there is that explains why birds and planes can fly. So why don't we ever hear disputes about the existence of gravity even though there's air and space travel? Perhaps because there are no conservative think tanks or corporations dedicated to fostering a culture of gravity denial. A belief in the science of gravity, of course, has no adverse monetary impact on corporate profits, nor personal livelihoods and lifestyles. And unlike climate change, the activities that contribute to gravity do not need to be drastically slowed and eventually eviscerated to preserve sentient existence on the planet.

When humans achieved flight, and eventually space travel, they did so by circumventing gravity, not by defeating it. Climate denial, especially in the age of Trump, must be approached in the same vein, and this is best done through effective storytelling that contributes to effective action. Because unlike facts and science, news reports and political speeches, stories are not accepted or rejected—they are absorbed and allowed to diffuse into our emotional consciousness. Many times, this can mobilize people and effect change—which was the case with stories like *Silent Spring* (Carson, 1962), *Uncle Tom's Cabin* (Stowe, 1852) and the transmission of civil rights abuses in the Jim Crow South.

But *Intentional Circumvention* is not just about stories. It's also about the kinds of stories, the stories that embrace getting to the *Yes*, while also portraying how we depart from the *No*. As Hoffman reminds us, the messenger is as important as the message; we must be mindful of the process that developed the message; we must choose messages that are accessible; and we must present solutions that offer a vision of the future we all collectively want. This is the process that allows us to become intentional circumvention practitioners who are portraying why we say yes to the world we want by caring for one another through simultaneous care for the only planet we can call home.

How we become intentional circumvention practitioners:

A snapshot of the regenerative agriculture movement

Whether you believe in climate change or not, no one can dispute the massive impacts that Hurricane Katrina, Superstorm Sandy and, more recently, Hurricane Maria had on lives, the economy and our thinking on the resiliency needed to deal with storms that powerful. But as Hoffman (2015) reports, the nexus established between Sandy and climate change was not afforded to Katrina. He is right to conclude that Katrina, which was a perfect storm of neglect, systemic racism and warming oceans, was not afforded the same discussions on climate because of New Orleans' demographics—very poor and Black. And Hoffman was also correct to assert that, *"events do not in of themselves create social change"* (p. 52).

I would take it a step further and assert that reactions to specific *climate events*, whether they be *"natural"* disasters, political appointments or policy announcements, will also not create social change. Rather, they tend to simply continue the current debate on climate science, both sides of the issue firmly entrenched in their respective fox holes. This may work for building email lists and fundraising, but it's not an effective praxis for circumventing climate denial and bringing people together. Further, as Hoffman points out, reactionary messaging bereft of a human connection may increase social fission and *"animate our emerging social schism"* due to distrust (2015, p. 26).

Reactionary messaging to so-called shock events too often neglects *intersectionality*, which is an important variable of the overall climate fight and a necessary component for effective storytelling. Scholar Kimberle' Crenshaw in 1989 who coined the phrase, declared that *"intersectionality lies in the recognition that multiple oppressions are not each suffered separately but rather as a single, synthesized experience"* (Smith, 2013, par 15). To this end, we must move beyond portraying climate change solely through a lens of rising seas, heat shocks, and polar bears. Climate change is a system of oppression formed at the intersection of myriad forms of injustice impacting race, ethnicity, financial status, and gender/gender identity. For environmental and other NGOs that form the non-profit industrial apparatus, this represents an inconvenient truth that too often shows in their messaging and communications, which seldom focuses primarily on marginalized people most impacted by the climate crisis. This is especially apparent for the climate action "movement" and its historically white-led groups who would do well to heed the words of Ed Miller, Environmental Program Manager of the Joyce Foundation, who states, "we're not going to make big changes in climate as long as climate is seen solely as an environmental issue."

Current messaging models, not rooted in intersectionality, have not only created silos, which can also be characterized as firm if not obstinate single issues, existing not only outside of the *"movement,"* but also within it. This silos within silo situation has bifurcated environmentalists who are identified by specific environmental issues such as *fracktivist, environmental justice (EJ) group,* and *divestment movement.* Until these inter-and intra-social movement silos are busted up, we will not be able to tell effective stories that circumvent climate denialism. Communicating with an intersectional lens makes us better storytellers in itself, because it forces us to increase our focus on people instead of solely focusing on parts per million, sea level rise, and degrees increase, which can be above the layperson's ahead and act as a buffer for transformational communication necessary to mobilize the maximum number of people to embark in climate action.

One of the most effective tools for circumventing, if not altogether eviscerating, distrust is effective storytelling. The climate action "movement" must first deal with its issues of intersectionality before it can become an effective storytelling machine. To this end, I would argue that we must shed this idea of a "Shock Doctrine" and embrace a *"Doctrine of the Status Quo."* Understanding the myriad events that perpetuate injustice in this way, as opposed to "shocks," will assist with reducing reactionary messaging to so-called shock events, which erect single-issue silos that act as anathema to an intersectional praxis Krenshaw prescribes for mutual and far-reaching justice.

As Klein reminds us, *"A state of shock is produced when a story is ruptured... Trump is not a rupture at all, but rather the culmination – the logical end point – of a great many dangerous stories our culture has been telling for a very long time"* (p. 257) She is correct, and due to decades old reports from the *Kerner Report,* to *Toxic Waste and Race,* to years of research from scholars including Dr. Beverly Wright and Dr. Robert Bullard, I would posit that we no longer have the right to be shocked by any of the events we witness associated with oppression and the accompanying climate crisis - which is not to say that we shouldn't be collectively outraged.

But how we react and communicate this outrage has serious implications for whether we establish and maintain efficacy in our struggle for mutual justice. Reactionary messaging to single events, each individual act of this president or a single piece of fossil fuel infrastructure without articulating how they all operate in concert only reinforces existing silos and creates even more work for a climate "movement" as it pertains to outreach and galvanization of a broad movement of people from diverse backgrounds. For a guild of organizations stressing the need for greater energy efficiency, the climate "movement," at times, operates in a way that's antithetical to one of their chief paradigms. Ineffective communication through storytelling bereft of maximum intersectionality is a major reason for this – and it must be addressed quickly.

This is where one of the most imperative tools for better storytelling comes into play. Narrative Power Analysis (NPA) works from the premise that what makes for powerful stories are not facts alone, but the ability of the story to, *"create meaning in the minds and hearts of the listeners"* (Reinsborough, & Canning, n.d., par 3). Taking the example of Katrina, it could be argued that it was the stories of the people most impacted depicted in movies like *When the Levees Broke* (Lee, 2006) and television series like *Treme* (Hemingway et al., 2010) that better portrayed the devastation that impacted New Orleans, when compared to news reports, and certainly vacuous speeches offered by George W. Bush and mayor Ray Nagen.

As Paul Van De Carr reminds us in *Storytelling and Social Change* (2015) that people don't relate to issues. Instead, they relate to other people's stories. And once one understands another, they can identify a shared vision for a better world and work to make it a reality. This statement speaks to the *Yes*, which must be included in our communications moving forward. Storytelling must be our primary method for injecting new urgency and bold ideas into confronting the intersecting crises of climate change, racism and inequality.

For the last two years, I have been working with a diverse coalition including Native Americans, rural farmers, social justice advocates, scientists and environmentalists called, "RegeNErate Nebraska." The goals of the group include fostering a massive transformation from the corporate, "degenerative" agricultural model, to a regenerative model that focuses on soil health, ethical treatment of livestock and access to affordable, nutritious food. Moreover, the coalition calls for a massive decentralization of the food system in a way that sustains the financial viability of small family farms and fosters economic stability for rural, Tribal and urban communities. The added bonus, if you will, is that the Regenerative Ag model serves as a working solution to the climate crisis by using no pesticides and emphasizing regeneration of soil through a massive reduction in soil tillage, which in turn allows for the soil to act as a natural carbon dioxide sink via biosequestration. According to the "4 For 1,000" initiative, a global regenerative agriculture platform, an increase of soil sequestration capacity of just 0.4% annually of the 5 billion hectares of global agricultural lands would facilitate the storage of 6 gigatons of carbon dioxide back in the soil (Tickell, 2017 p. 26).

Those involved in the work of coalition building understand the myriad challenges associated with fusing seemingly disparate interests into a collective framework that benefits each group mutually and simultaneously. The groups and individuals who first formed RegeNErate Nebraska understood that mollifying these challenges was a primary and essential step to foster and maintain an efficacious coalition. We also understood that the process of busting single-issue silos actually required a process of entering each silo individually in order to draw them to an eventual intersection. And, perhaps most important, we studied theories that examined the failures of previous "movements" from achieving their ultimate goals.

Arguably the best explanation was provided by former SNCC organizer and Black liberation advocate Kwame Ture (formerly known as Stokely Carmichael). In his epochal work, *Black Power: The Politics of Liberation*, Ture explains, "*The major mistake made by exponents of the coalition theory is that they advocate alliances with groups which have never had as their central goal the necessarily total revamping of the society*" (Ture 1967, p.60). Ture's assertion was key for our coalition, because our work involves a massive transformation from the current agricultural model, which serves a few corporations at the expense of the many.

Additionally, because our coalition is comprised of a diverse set of backgrounds, races, ethnicities and experiences, we embraced Ture's admonishment of conforming to an Anglo-centric position as it pertains to our messaging and operations. Ture explains, "*We do not believe it possible to form a meaningful coalition unless both or all parties are not only willing but believe it absolutely necessary to challenge Anglo-Conformity and other prevailing norms and institutions…The Anglo-conformity position assumes that what is good for American whites is good for Black people [and all people]*" (Ture p.62). Taking these lessons into account, we decided to tell each other our individual stories in an effort to develop a mutual, intersectional and collective narrative that we would share with the larger public through a series of Regenerative workshops statewide.

Andrew Hoffman instructs us to utilize messaging that is "personally accessible" stating, "people respond to what's salient and personal" (2015, p. 59). At the same time, he admonishes us to move beyond focusing on the *No*. "*Cataclysmic scenarios can become 'deactivating' for people, not just by evoking dismissal, but also leaving people without a sense of sense of hope for a solution*" (Hoffman, 2015, p. 59). To this end, RegeNERate Nebraska designed a narrative that first aimed to portray the various challenges each coalition member is experiencing or experienced under the Degenerative Ag model. We believed this was necessary to engender a process of galvanizing attention and inviting the many people experiencing similar challenges to the discussion. At the same time, we took Hoffman's "cataclysmic scenario" admonishment to heart, using the successes of the Regenerative Ag transformation –the *Yes*- as a key variable of our story telling. Finally, we created a document entitled, *Regeneration Proclamation* so that interested parties could take the story home with them and share it with their friends, families and neighbors *(RegeNErate Nebraska, n.d.)*.

Perhaps the most effective variable of the RegeNErate Nebraska story is that it largely focuses on the people and tells the story of the challenges in each representative community and how they intersect with one another. We're telling the story of how to get from the world as it is—the *No*—to the world we want and know we can have—the *Yes*. This idea of focusing on the *Yes* is not as new as it is more necessary than at any moment in history. Our ideas are catching on as communities from states as close as Iowa and countries as far away as Nicaragua are soliciting us to bring our story to them, so that they can take germane elements and apply them to their specific situations.

What's even more encouraging about our coalition is the fact that we rarely discuss climate change in itself. I honestly don't even know if all of our partners believe in or are as concerned with the climate crisis as others, and it doesn't matter because the RegeNErate story is rooted in mutual justice, which just so happens to provide an actual solution to climate change through collective impact. This represents the epitome of *Intentional Circumvention*, addressing a controversial challenge like climate change, without struggling with each other over whether it exists, or the best way to address it.

Conclusion

We all need to become the best intentional circumvention practitioners as possible. We're out of time to debate the science, fight over the best approaches, or whether climate change even exists. We don't have time to react solely to Trump or climate denialists. This time is better spent increasing our capacity for effective storytelling that busts silos by focusing on the most important parts of climate change: the people who are being impacted by it and the tactics, organizing, and ideas they unleash to address it. This is how we circumvent climate denialists while mobilizing people to act on climate change through an intersectional lens.

We can dispatch of climate denial in the age of Trump, and beyond, by going around it and him simultaneously—and that will be such a great people-oriented, intersectional, and silo-busting story to tell for sure. Because at the end of the day it's not just one man we have to confront, it's an entire system and circumference of injustice that led to his ascension in the first place. I think Charlene Carruthers in her latest work, *Unapologetic: A Black, Queer and Feminist Mandate for Radical Movements*, portrays the power and importance of storytelling, proclaiming, "If the relationship between two people is one of the smallest units of movement building, then the stories we hear and share within those relationships are the springboards for action" (Carruthers, 2018, p. 44).

May our stories reduce the distance between justice and injustice in a way that allows everyone to hear, comprehend and act on them so that we arrive at the world we want and know is possible.

References

Aikido, Judo, Jujitsu and Karate - Comparing different martial arts. (2008). Retrieved from http://www.alljujitsu.com/jujitsu.html

Banerjee, N., Song, L., & Hasemyer, D. (2015, September 16). Exxon: The road not taken. Retrieved from http://insideclimatenews.org/content/exxon-the-road-not-taken.

Carrington, D. (2015, January 7). Leave fossil fuels buried to prevent climate change, study urges. *The Guardian.* Retrieved from https://www.theguardian.com/environment/2015/jan/07/much-worlds-fossil-fuel-reserve-must-stay-buried-prevent-climate-change-study-says

Carruthers, C. A. (2018). *Unapologetic: A black, queer and feminist mandate for radical movements.* Boston, MA: Beacon Press.

Carson, R. (2002). *Silent spring* (Anniversary edition). Boston, MA: Houghton Mifflin.

Cook, J. (2017). What does past climate change tell us about global warming? Retrieved from https://www.skepticalscience.com/climate-change-little-ice-age-medieval-warm-period.htm

Covington, S. (1997). *Moving a public policy agenda: The strategic philanthropy of conservative foundations.* Washington, D.C: National Committee for Responsive Philanthropy. Retrieved from https://www.ncrp.org/publication/moving-public-policy-agenda

Dickinson, T. (2007, June 28). Six years of deceit: Inside the Bush Administration's secret campaign to deny global Warming. *Rolling Stone.* Retrieved from http://www.rollingstone.com/politics/news/six-years-of-deceit-20070628

Hayes, (2014, April 22). The new abolitionism - Averting planetary disaster will mean forcing fossil fuel companies to give up at least $10 trillion in wealth.

The Nation. Retrieved from https://www.thenation.com/article/new-abolitionism/

Hemingway, A., Simon, D., Overmyer, E., Alexander, K., Brown, R., Dickens, K., ... & Attias, D. (Producers). (2010). *Treme.* [Television series]. New York, NY: HBO

Hoffman, A. J. (2015). *How culture shapes the climate change debate* (1st ed.). Palo Alto, California: Stanford Briefs.

Holmberg, J., & Robert, K. H. (2000). Backcasting — a framework for strategic planning. *International Journal of Sustainable Development & World Ecology, 7*(4), 291–308. https://doi.org/10.1080/13504500009470049

INCITE! (2017). *The revolution will not be funded: Beyond the non-profit industrial complex.* Durham, North Carolina: Duke University Press.

Klein, N. (2017). *No Is not enough: Resisting Trump's shock politics and winning the world we need.* Chicago, IL: Haymarket Books.

Lee, S. (Director). Lee, S., & Pollard, S. D. (Producers). (2006). When the levees broke: A requiem in four acts [Television series]. New York, NY: HBO

Lewis, R. (2014, August 14). Ferguson reports raise questions on media criminalization of blacks. *Aljazeera.* Retrieved from http://america.aljazeera.com/articles/2014/8/14/ferguson-media-iftheygunnedmedown.html

Nixon, R. (2013). *Slow violence and the environmentalism of the poor.* Cambridge, MA: Harvard University Press.

RegeNErate Nebraska (n.d.). Regeneration proclamation - Growing Nebraska's communities from the soil up [Brochure]. Retrieved from https://docs.wixstatic.com/ugd/181ce8_b49d503b832b4a4db3b93136c3883 850.pdf

Reinsborough, P. & Canning, D. (n.d.). Theory: Narrative power analysis. *Beautiful* Trouble. Retrieved from http://beautifultrouble.org/theory/narrative-power-analysis/

Smith, S. (2013) Black feminism and intersectionality. *International Socialist Review, 94.* Retrieved from https://isreview.org/issue/91/black-feminism-and-intersectionality

Stowe, H. B. (2005). *Uncle Tom's cabin* (1st ed.). Mineola, NY: Dover Thrift Editions.

Tickell, Josh (2017). *Kiss the ground: How the food you eat can reverse climate change, heal your body & ultimately save the world.* New York, NY. Simon and Schuster, Inc.

Ture, Kwame & Hamilton, Charles V. (1967). *Black power: The politics of liberation.* New York, NY. Random House Books.

Van De Carr, P. (2015). Storytelling and social change: A guide for activists, organization and social entrepreneurs. Working Narratives. Retrieved from http://workingnarratives.org/wp-content/uploads/2016/02/story-guide-second-edition.pdf

Chapter 4

Fire, Ice or Drought?
Picturing Humanity
in Climate Change Imagery

Kim Sheehan, PhD, Nicole Dahmen, PhD and David L. Morris II, PhD

Introduction

Global climate change is real, man-made, and measurable (van der Linden, Leiserowitz, Rosenthal, & Maibach, 2017). Our planet is experiencing increases in air and water temperatures, intense drought and forest fires, widespread melting of snow and ice, and rising levels of the ocean—all evidence of the effects of change in climate, and all potentially devastating to life (NASA, 2017). Yet, only three percent of Americans listed "environment/pollution" as the most important issue in 2016—the lowest of twenty-five different issues throughout the year (Gallup, 2016). Additionally, when concerns are expressed, polls show that climate change is a more polarizing issue than gay marriage or abortion (Roser-Renouf, Maibach, Leiserowitz, & Rosenthal, 2016).

Why the lack of concern regarding climate change? Some research suggests that the messaging—both text and visuals—being used in both public communication advocacy campaigns and news media coverage of climate change often does not resonate with audiences (Hansen & Machin, 2008; Hart & Feldman, 2016). While text is often the focus of news analysis and effects research, scholars suggest that it is equally important to consider the growing role of visuals in the media—especially in regard to climate change (Hart & Feldman, 2016).

One of the standard images used to represent climate change is its effect on polar bears (Prisco, 2016). Despite the ubiquity of images of a lone polar bear on disappearing ice, it is not an image that necessarily connects with a human audience given the lack of portrayals of climate change's effect on people. Regarding reporting about climate change, Josh Haner, a New York Times Pulitzer prize-winning visual journalist argues, "It's my opinion that people have become numb to the stereotypic climate change/global warming photos of a polar bear on a tiny piece of ice" (personal communication, May 5, 2016). Considering his own reporting about climate change, Haner states, "What I'm aiming to do is to create imagery that makes people think and care enough to invest in reading our story and empathize with the people who are being affected right now" (personal communication, May 5, 2016).

Perhaps, as Haner suggested, the stereotypical climate images that people see on a regular basis have little effect on their perceptions of the seriousness of climate change. This exploratory study tests this assumption empirically using a 3x3x2 experimental design to examine what types of photographs relating to climate change have the best potential to connect with people on an emotional level and systematically assesses the degree to which the type of climate change effect (forest fire, melting ice, extreme drought), inclusion of people (no people, small group, individual), and locality of the climate effect (domestic or global) affects emotions and engagement.

Literature review

Global climate change is real, man-made, and measurable (van der Linden et al., 2017). Our planet is experiencing increases in air and water temperatures, intense drought and forest fires, widespread melting of snow and ice, and rising levels of the ocean—all evidence of the effects of change in climate, and all potentially devastating to life (NASA, 2017). Yet, only three percent of Americans listed "environment/pollution" as the most important issue in 2016—the lowest of twenty-five different issues throughout the year (Gallup, 2016). Additionally, when concerns are expressed, polls show that climate change is a more polarizing issue than gay marriage or abortion (Roser-Renouf et al., 2016).

Why the lack of concern regarding climate change? Some research suggests that the messaging—both text and visuals—being used in both public communication advocacy campaigns and news media coverage of climate change often does not resonate with audiences (Hansen & Machin, 2008; Hart & Feldman, 2016). While text is often the focus of news analysis and effects research, scholars suggest that it is equally important to consider the growing role of visuals in the media—especially in regard to climate change (Hart & Feldman, 2016).

One of the standard images used to represent climate change is its effect on polar bears (Prisco, 2016). Despite the ubiquity of images of a lone polar bear on disappearing ice, it is not an image that necessarily connects with a human audience given the lack of portrayals of climate change's effect on people. Regarding reporting about climate change, Josh Haner, a New York Times Pulitzer prize-winning visual journalist argues, "It's my opinion that people have become numb to the stereotypic climate change/global warming photos of a polar bear on a tiny piece of ice" (personal communication, May 5, 2016).

Considering his own reporting about climate change, Haner states, "What I'm aiming to do is to create imagery that makes people think and care enough to invest in reading our story and empathize with the people who are being affected right now" (personal communication, May 5, 2016).

Perhaps, as Haner suggested, the stereotypical climate images that people see on a regular basis have little effect on their perceptions of the seriousness of climate change. This exploratory study tests this assumption empirically using a 3x3x2 experimental design to examine what types of photographs relating to climate change have the best potential to connect with people on an emotional level and systematically assesses the degree to which the type of climate change effect (forest fire, melting ice, extreme drought), inclusion of people (no people, small group, individual), and locality of the climate effect (domestic or global) affects emotions and engagement.

Photojournalism and emotional reaction

In his seminal work *Public Opinion*, Walter Lippmann wrote, "...what each man does is based not on direct and certain knowledge, but on pictures made by himself or given to him" (Lippmann, 1922, p. 16). Those pictures—whether they be images of climate change or some other pressing issue—come directly from the mass media. News media photographs can influence how audiences understand news topics. Photographs explain and illustrate news stories, giving readers an entry point for news coverage, as well as conveying information visually (Garcia, 2002). Regarding news content, King and Lester (2005) showed that newspaper photographs often generate a stronger public reaction than the corresponding written stories. Research has demonstrated that news stories are more likely to be placed on the front page—a place of prominence and authority– if they have a compelling photograph (Moeller, 1999). Visual coverage has now become essential to reporting news, in comparison to early newspapers' usage of visuals as supportive content for the written story (King & Lester, 2005; Moeller, 1999).

Photographs can have a high level of influence on viewers, particularly if they contain content about news. Previous research has clearly shown that the inclusion of a photograph with a news story increases audience attention to the story (Adam, Quinn, & Edmonds, 2007). In addition, previous research has indicated that pictures are easier to recall than words (Paivio, Rogers, & Smythe, 1968). Lester (2005), among others, has argued that the study of images in media provides a rich avenue for research.

Maier, Slovic, and Mayorga (2016) argue that news content must connect with audiences on an emotional level. Their research shows that two factors significantly influence emotional connection and subsequent audience reaction: story personification (giving a difficult news story a "human face") and stories with photographic images (Maier et al., 2016). News images from Vietnam—for example, the iconic image of a young girl badly burned by Napalm—have been described by scholars as emotional catalysts for ending the Vietnam War (Kumar, 2006; Louw, 2003).

What makes photographs influential is "...the high drama and emotional pull of symbolic moments of death, sacrifice, and patriotism" (Griffin, 1999, p. 129). Images have been shown to evoke instant emotional reactions among their viewers and to possess an "attention grabbing capacity" (Ewbank, Barnard, Croucher, Ramponi, & Calder, 2009, p. 127), which can leave a lasting impression. The underlying supposition is that photos such as the one described above from Vietnam hold power to move audiences from complacency to action. Emotional reactions such as this happen on a visceral level, where memorable images with an impact produce a greater response (Ewbank et al., 2009). The ability to focus on direct horrific effects to *one* individual—as opposed to groups of people—has also been shown by psychological research to increase empathy (Västfjäll, Slovic, Mayorga, & Peters, 2014). In addition, the photo described above from Vietnam focuses on one individual and shows the effects of war on her life, thus creating the "story personification" effect (Maier et al., 2016). The current study aims to add to the theoretical understanding of the effects of images regarding emotional reaction and public opinion.

Imagery in climate change reporting

Research has suggested that news reporting of climate change often includes visuals. These visuals frequently show the effects of climate change (O'Neill & Smith, 2014) and often include scientists and politicians, as opposed to individuals who are experiencing direct effects from climate change (Hart & Feldman, 2016). Additional content analysis has shown that regarding climate change imagery in news reporting, few stories include mitigation imagery (that is, imagery that shows a response to address climate change as opposed to negative effects of climate change) (O'Neill, 2013). Regarding effects, images of flooded homes, for example, have been shown to capture audience attention and elevate perceived issue importance (O'Neill & Nicholson-Cole, 2009). In a subsequent study, Hart and Feldman (2016) also found that an aerial image of flooding had an impact in affecting perceived issue importance. However, while attention-grabbing, these types of "fear"-based imagery have been shown to lower efficacy (O'Neill & Nicholson-Cole, 2009). An image that has been shown to lead to an increased sense of efficacy was an image of a solar panel, rather than an image of a smokestack or flood (Hart & Feldman, 2016). Despite these findings, Hart and Feldman (2016) suggest that it is still an "open research question" as to perceived issue importance and efficacy effects of both imagery and text on diverse groups of people (p. 420).

Indeed, climate change is a critical topic. Academics must continue to explore reporting and effects regarding climate change to fully understand which types of messages resonate with audiences. The current study brings together existing theory on the knowledge-deficit model and research findings on both climate change imagery and journalistic imagery in general to examine what types of photographs relating to climate change have the best potential to connect with people on an emotional level and systematically assesses the degree to which the type of climate change effect (forest fire, melting ice, extreme drought), inclusion of people (no people, small group, individual), and locality of the climate effect (domestic or international) affects emotions and engagement in order identify the types of images that will encourage people to learn more about climate change and act accordingly. Based on the exploratory nature of this research, we propose the following research questions:

RQ1: Do images of different types of climate change effects (forest fire, melting ice, extreme drought) generate different levels of emotion and engagement?

RQ2: Building off Leisorowitz's (2007) finding that local and regional threats to the environment tend to be more salient than global threats, do images of climate change events that occur closer geographically to the viewer generate different levels of emotion and engagement than images that are not geographically close?

RQ3: Do images of climate change events containing people generate different levels of emotion and engagement than images that do not contain people? Does whether the people are pictured in small groups or individuals affect emotion and engagement?

RQ4: What specific images generate the highest levels of emotion and engagement, and does this vary by event?

Method

To answer the research questions, researchers conducted an experiment to assess how people respond to different images of climate change. The stimulus condition was a news photograph with an associated caption. This 3x3x2 experimental design was developed to examine what types of photographs relating to climate change have the best potential to connect with people on an emotional level and systematically assesses the degree to which the type of climate change effect (forest fire, melting ice, extreme drought), inclusion of people (no people, small group, individual), and locality of the climate effect (domestically or internationally) affects emotions (specifically, the degree to which they feel compassionate and sympathetic after viewing the image) and engagement (specifically, the degree to which they experienced an emotional response and could picture themselves in the image, believe the story is relevant and could change their life) using a 5-point scale where 1=not at all and 5=very much so. Constructs of emotion and engagement to visual imagery have been utilized by Maier et al. (2016), McIntyre and Sobel (2017), Myrick and Evans (2017) and Oliver, Dillard, Bae and Tamul (2012).

Again, there are known and proven effects of climate change, notably extreme weather and such direct effects such as flooding, melting ice, droughts, and forest fires (NASA, 2017). Because images of flooding have been studied to a large degree (Hart & Feldman, 2016; O'Neill & Nicholson-Cole, 2009), the current research focused on images of understudied climate effects, specifically forest fires, melting ice, and extreme drought. Researchers also selected images of melting ice to look at imagery beyond that of a lone polar bear on a disappearing ice floe. Based on existing research findings on story personification (putting a human face on a story) and story portrayals of individuals versus groups (Maier et al., 2016), researchers selected three different images to manipulate the presence or absence of people in images for each of the three climate events: climate event with no people; climate event with the inclusion of a small group of people; climate event with the inclusion and focus on one person. In addition, to account for story personification, the caption for the images of a climate event with the inclusion and focus on one person also identified the one person by name and age.

To assess the degree of the effects of locality, research also manipulated the image captions for the site of occurrence that stated whether or not the image was taken domestically (within the United States) or internationally (outside of the United States). With the exception of manipulation for story personification and locality, the captions for each of the three climate effects were the same and connected to the type of effect. Thus, for each of the three climate events, six different images with captions were tested. See Table 4.1 for a summary of images and captions.

Table 4.1 Photographs used as stimuli

Fire			
Event	*Event with no people*	*Event with small group*	*Event with individual*
Image description	Landscape of burnt trees	Landscape of burnt trees with group of hikers in the distance	Landscape of a forest on fire with silhouette of one individual in lower right-hand corner
*Caption: domestic**	Charred trees in Southeast Alaska. Climate change is a prime suspect in a rise of wildfires in the boreal forest.	Charred trees in Southeast Alaska. Climate change is a prime suspect in a rise of wildfires in the boreal forest	Andrew McLaughlin lost his home in a forest fire in Southeast Alaska. Climate change is a prime suspect in a rise of wildfires in the boreal forest
*Caption: global**	Charred trees in Alberta, Canada. Climate change is a prime suspect in a rise of wildfires in the boreal forest	Charred trees in Alberta, Canada. Climate change is a prime suspect in a rise of wildfires in the boreal forest	Andrew McLaughlin lost his home in a forest fire in Alberta, Canada. Climate change is a prime suspect in a rise of wildfires in the boreal forest
Melting Ice			
Event	*Event with no people*	*Event with small group*	*Event with individual*
Image description	Landscape of ice sheet	Landscape of ice sheet with people in the distance	Individual on a melting ice sheet
*Caption: domestic**	Ice sheets in Alaska are melting at alarming rates	Ice sheets in Alaska are melting at alarming rates	Albert Lukas's world is melting around him. Ice sheets in Alaska are melting at alarming rates
*Caption: global**	Ice sheets in the Arctic are melting at alarming rates	Ice sheets in the Arctic are melting at alarming rates	Albert Lukas's world is melting around him. Ice sheets in the Arctic are melting at alarming rates.
Extreme draught			
Event	*Event with no people*	*Event with small group*	*Event with individual*
Image description	Drought ravaged landscape.	Drought landscape with two people walking away from the camera toward a house	Drought landscape with woman and child in foreground

*Caption: domestic**	The dry earth in Yuma, Arizona.	To some children, the extreme drought in Yuma, Arizona no long-er makes the town feel like home.	Agustina Moya with her 2-year old daughter in the ruins of a family house caused the ex-treme drought in Yuma, Arizona.
*Caption: global**	The dry earth in Llapallapani, Bolivia	To some children, the extreme drought in Llapallapani, Bolivia no longer makes the town feel like home.	Agustina Moya with her 2-year old daughter in the ruins of a family house caused the ex-treme drought in Llapal-lapani, Bolivia

*All captions included "Around the globe, governments are confronting the reality that as human-caused climate change warms the planet, melting ice sheets, rising sea levels, increased flooding, harsher droughts, and forest fires are causing immediate effects, driving people from their homes."

Participants were recruited for this study through two channels: first, through the snowball method and second, through Amazon's Mechanical Turk. Researchers utilized the snowball method by posting invitations on social media sites and asking people to participate and also share the post. Both the snowball method and Amazon Mechanical Turk represent convenience samples and are limited in their generalizability to larger populations. However, as we wanted to look at differences at how individuals react to different stimuli, a convenience sample was appropriate. By combining two different convenience samples, we attempted to minimize any biases inherent in either sample (Casebeer & Verhoef, 1997).

Respondents were asked about their emotional connection to the image by asking the degree to which the image made them feel compassionate and sympathetic (Maier et al., 2016) utilizing a 5-point scale (1=not at all, 5=very much so). Respondents were asked about their engagement with the image by responding to how well they could 1) picture themselves in the image, 2) believe the story associated with the image would change their life, 3) believe the story associated with the image would be relevant to their life and 4) experience an emotional response to the image, using the same five-point scale (Oliver et al., 2012). Finally, respondents provided demographic information. Data were analyzed in SPSS using t-tests and ANOVAs to test for differences between conditions.

A total of 237 individuals participated in the experiment (40% from snowball sample, 60% from MTurk sample). About 47% identified as male and 53% as female; about 89% identified their race as white, 5.5% as Asian, 3% as Native American, 1% as Black, and 4.5% as 'other.' About a third (31%)

reported earning a Bachelor's degree and another third (34%) reported earning an advanced degree. Respondents' ages ranged from 19 to 76 years old, with an average respondent age of 40. Respondents came from 36 out of 50 states plus the District of Columbia. Although this is not a generalizable sample, it does reflect a diverse range of demographics providing value for an exploratory study.

Findings

When given a range of current issues and asked about the importance of the issues to the respondent's daily life, respondents indicated that of the seven issues provided, climate change was least important (mean level of importance=2.3 where 1=not at all important and 5=highly important). Most important to the respondents was the Israeli-Palestinian conflict (mean=3.33), immigration (mean=2.82), unemployment (mean=2.78), global economic stagnation (mean=2.76), domestic violence (mean=2.59) and crime (mean=2.51). Importance of climate change is significantly lower than the importance of crime ($t=3.2588$, $p=.0012$), mirroring other studies that show that climate change is not a priority for most Americans.

The two statements about emotions were summed (Cronbach's alpha=.92) and the four statements about engagement were likewise summed (Cronbach's alpha=.71) in order to create the emotion and engagement scales for analysis. Both alpha scores meet the level of acceptability as suggested by DeVellis (2012).

The first research question asked whether different images of climate change events stimulate different levels of emotion and engagement. To answer this question, we calculated a mean score for emotion and engagement for all six photographs for each type of event (forest fire, melting ice, extreme drought), excluding all other variables to get an overall score for each type of event. As seen in Table 4.2, the data show that highest levels of both emotion and engagement were garnered by the forest fire images, while the extreme drought and melting ice images were equal in terms generating emotion and engagement.

Given that differences exist by the type of climate change effect (forest fire, melting ice, extreme drought), we examine the other research questions regarding international or domestic and present/absence of people by event.

Table 4.2 Average Scores for Emotion and Engagement by Event

Event	Average Emotion	Average Engagement
Drought	11.19	12.43
Fire	11.71	13.14
Melting ice	10.84	12.56

Notes: Anova emotion: F=4.284, df=799, p=.0146. Anova engagement: F=3.175, df=799, p=.030. Post hoc tests show that 'Fire' is significantly higher than 'Drought' and 'Ice'.

Images of extreme drought

Responses for extreme drought are displayed on Table 4.3. The second research question asked whether images of climate change events that occur closer geographically to the viewer generate different levels of emotion and engagement than images that are not geographically close? To answer this, we calculated an overall mean score emotion and engagement for the three international and three domestic frames for extreme drought. For emotion, the international images of extreme drought reported a significantly higher score (mean-3.42) than the domestic images (mean=2.78, t = 9.9106, p<.0001). For engagement, the domestic images of extreme drought reported a significantly higher score (mean=3.17) than the international images (mean=3.04) (t=2.1667, p=.021).

The third research question asked about the effects of including people in images about climate change. We also examined whether pictures of individuals or pictures of small groups of people influenced emotions and engagement differently. Table 4.2 provides results of an ANOVA of the presence of people in the image. This shows that significant differences do exist in terms of emotional response: ad hoc tests showing that the images showing individual people generated the highest level of emotion (mean=3.77 for international images and 3.70 for domestic images); both of these were significantly higher than the images with small groups of people (mean=3.36 for international images and 3.16 for domestic images) and images with no people generated the lowest levels (mean=3.16 for international images and 2.91 for domestic images, ANOVA F=11.737, p<.0001). For engagement, the opposite relationship was seen. Images without people scored significantly higher (mean=3.20 for international images and 3.40 for domestic images) than the other images (F=2.734, p=.02).

Overall, the images that generated the highest levels of emotion were those of the international and domestic drought event that included an individual. These images generated higher mean scores than the image with the next highest score (T 5.23 p<.000). The image that generated the highest levels of engagement was the photograph of a domestic drought event that did not include people; the mean score was higher than that of the image with the next highest mean score (T= 2.923 p=.004).

Table 4.3 Extreme Drought: Emotion and Engagement

	Global				Local			
Presence of people	None	Small group	Individual		None	Small group	Individual	
Compassionate	3.06	3.4	3.73		2.88	3.13	3.79	
Sympathetic	3.13	3.33	3.82		2.94	3.20	3.79	
Average emotion*	**3.16**	**3.36**	**3.77**	**3.42**	**2.91**	**3.16**	**3.70**	**2.78**
Picture yourself in the image	2.97	2.93	2.20		3.12	3.14	2.35	
Believe story associated with image would change your life	3.06	2.66	2.88		3.31	2.68	2.88	
Believe story associated with image would be relevant to your life	3.41	2.69	3.11		3.59	3.17	3.35	
Experience an emotional response to the photograph	3.34	3.36	3.91		3.59	3.17	3.74	
Average engagement**	**3.20**	**2.91**	**3.00**	**3.04***	**3.40**	**3.11**	**3.08**	**3.17***

Notes: *For emotion Global was significantly higher than Local (t = 9.9106 , p<.0001); engagement, Local was significant higher than global (t=2.1667, p=.021).

*Anova for inclusion/exclusion of people for emotion, F=11.737, p<.0001. Mean score for local with individual and global with no people were higher than all other scores.

**Anova for inclusion/exclusion of people for engagement, F=2.734, p=.02. Mean score for Local with no people was higher than mean score for global with a small group of people and individual person.

Images of forest fires

Responses for forest fires are displayed on Table 4.4 The second research question asked whether images of climate change events that occur closer geographically to the viewer generate different levels of emotion and engagement than images that are not geographically close? To answer this, we calculated an overall mean score emotion and engagement for the three international and three domestic frames for the forest fire images and found there were no significant difference between the overall emotion scores and engagement scores between the international and domestic frames.

Table 4.4 Forest Fire: Emotion and Engagement

	Global				Local			
Presence of people	None	Small group	Individual		None	Small group	Individual	
Compassionate	3.18	3.28	3.45		3.00	3.15	3.66	
Sympathetic	3.15	3.28	3.60		3.15	3.09	3.64	
Average emotion*	**3.17**	**3.28**	**3.52**	**3.32**	**3.07**	**3.12**	**3.65**	**3.26**
Picture yourself in the image	2.75	2.78	2.88		2.75	3.09	2.82	
Believe story associated with image would change your life	3.21	3.21	3.40		3.125	3.15	3.24	
Believe story associated with image would be relevant to your life	3.50	3.28	3.31		3.28	3.46	3.34	
Experience an emotional response to the photograph	3.72	3.75	3.80		3.59	3.43	4.00	
Average engagement**	**3.30**	**3.25**	**3.34**	**3.29**	**3.18**	**3.28**	**3.35**	**3.27**

Notes: *ANOVA for presence of people for emotion measure: $F=7.162$, $df=197$, $p<.0001$.
**ANOVA was not significant.

The third research question asked whether the inclusion of people and whether the people are pictured in small groups or individuals influences emotions and engagement. Table 4.4 also provides results of an ANOVA of the presence of people in the image. This shows that significant differences do exist in terms of emotional engagement. Ad hoc tests showing that the images showing an individual person generated the highest level of emotion (mean=3.52 for international images and 3.61 for domestic images); both of these were significantly higher than the images with small groups of people (mean=3.25 for international images and 3.28 for domestic images) and images with no people generated the lowest levels (mean=3.17 for international images and 3.02 for domestic images, ANOVA F=7.162, df=232, p<.0001). For engagement, no significant differences were found.

Overall, the image that generated the highest levels of emotion was the image of the domestic forest fire event that included an individual person; the score was significantly higher than that of the next highest score (t=2, p=.046). For engagement, no significant differences were seen: all images generated the same level of engagement.

Images of melting ice

Responses for melting ice are displayed on Table 4.5 The second research question asked whether images of climate change events that occur closer geographically to the viewer generate different levels of emotion and engagement than images that are not geographically close. To answer this, we calculated an overall mean score emotion and engagement for the three international and three domestic frames for the melting ice images and found there was a significant difference in emotion between the international images (mean=2.92) and domestic images (mean=3.06, T=2.33, p=.02). There were no significant differences in the engagement scores between the international and domestic images.

The third research question asked whether the inclusion of people and whether the people are pictured in small groups or individuals influences emotions and engagement. Table 4.5 also provides results of an ANOVA of the presence of people in the image. This shows that significant differences do exist in terms of emotional engagement. Ad hoc tests showing that the domestic image showing an individual person generated the highest level of emotion (mean=3.64); this was significantly higher than the international images and the domestic image of a small group of people; the domestic image with no people reported the lowest level of emotion (ANOVA F=10.28, df=232, p<.0001). For engagement, no significant differences were found.

Table 4.5 Melting Ice: Emotion and Engagement

	Global				Local			
Presence of people	None	Small group	Individual		None	Small group	Individual	
Compassionate	2.72	2.93	3.17		2.47	3.02	3.66	
Sympathetic	2.65	2.90	3.21		2.48	3.07	3.62	
Average emotion*	**2.68**	**2.91**	**3.19**	**2.92**	**2.48**	**3.05**	**3.64**	**3.06**
Picture yourself in the image	2.46	2.65	2.36		2.41	2.77	2.97	
Believe story associated with image would change your life	3.44	3.22	3.00		2.97	3.25	3.17	
Believe story associated with image would be relevant to your life	3.47	3.45	3.21		3.05	3.51	3.49	
Experience an emotional response to the photograph	3.37	3.29	3.5		3.08	3.46	3.86	
Average engagement**	**3.19**	**3.15**	**3.02**	**3.11**	**2.88**	**3.25**	**3.37**	**3.17**

Notes: *ANOVA F=10.28, df=186, p<.0001. **ANOVA was not significant.

Overall, the domestic image picturing an individual generated the highest levels of emotion and engagement, with mean scores significantly higher than mean scores for the next highest image (for emotion, t=6.92, p<.0001, for engagement t=1.89, p=.048).

Table 4.6 provides a summary of the three analyses done on the different type of climate change effect (forest fire, melting ice, extreme drought) to assess any patterns. Whether an image is international or domestic seems to have some effects on levels of emotion and engagement, depending on the event. However, findings suggest that including images of an individual person generates consistently high levels of emotion and/or engagement, regardless of the context. In terms of trends regarding the highest scoring overall image, domestic images with an individual person represent three of the six highest scoring images.

Table 4.6 Summary of Trends

		Highest level: Global or local image	Highest level: People in image	Highest scoring image overall
Extreme Drought	Emotion	Global	**Individual person**	**Global with individual person**
	Engagement	Local	No consistent trends	Local image with no people
Forest Fire	Emotion	No difference	Individual person	Local and global image with individual person
	Engagement	No difference	No difference	No highest score
Melting Ice	Emotion	Local	Individual person	Local and individual person
	Engagement	No difference	Individual person	Local and individual person

Discussion

Despite the severity of the extreme weather events as a result of global climate change (van der Linden et al., 2017), the issue generally continues to be polarizing (Roser-Renouf et al., 2016) and to remain of low importance to many Americans (Gallup, 2016). Despite exposure to information about climate change, Americans still experience a knowledge deficit, suggesting that even though information is available, people tend to avoid attending to it. This may be because the messages of advocacy campaigns and news media coverage do not necessarily resonate with audiences. Regarding the imagery in these messages, audiences and those who report the news are beginning to suggest that one of the most stereotypical images of climate change—that of a lone polar bear on melting ice—does not resonate with a human audience (Haner, personal communication, May 5, 2016; Prisco, 2016). As related, research has suggested that audiences need to be able to establish an emotional connection with content (Bas & Grabe, 2015; Maier et al., 2016). Research has also shown that story personification and stories with photographic images can help audiences to connect with difficult news (Maier et al., 2016; Västfjäll et al., 2014).

Given the fact that visual coverage is essential to reporting news (King & Lester, 2005; Moeller, 1999) and that news stories with images increase audience attention to a news story (Adam et al., 2007), it is critical that academic scholarship examine the content and effects of images in the news media. In addition, regarding climate change imagery, scholars suggest that much more research is needed in this area (Hart & Feldman, 2016).

The intention of this exploratory study was to bring existing theory on the knowledge-deficit model and research findings on both climate change imagery and story personification to explore in a 3x3x2 experiment how photographs relating to climate change have the best potential to connect with people regarding emotion and engagement. To test this empirically, the stimulus materials were manipulated for the following variables to systematically assess the degree to which the type of climate change effect (forest fire, melting ice, extreme drought), the inclusion of people (no people, small group, individual), and the locality of the climate effect (domestic or internationally) affect emotions and engagement.

This study showed that images with an individual person (as opposed to a small group of people or no people) generated the strongest reactions from participants. This finding supports the research of previous scholars showing that story personification—with a focus on one individual—helps audiences to connect with the news (Maier et al., 2016; Västfjäll et al., 2014). Moreover, we used images that showed the individuals experiencing direct effects from climate change as opposed to individuals such as scientists or politicians (Hart & Feldman, 2016). Indeed, it was the images emphasizing humanity—as the individual effects on one person—that most connected with audiences.

The data provide mixed results depending on the climate change event pictured. This may suggest that it is the type of event, rather than where the event occurs, that is a stronger factor in creating an image that resonates with audiences. Additionally, depending on where someone lives in the United States, an image of an event such as melting ice is going to be seen as "far away" regardless of whether the ice is melting in Alaska or the South Pole.

Perhaps most important from a communications perspective is that this study showed that the type of climate change effect (forest fire, melting ice, extreme drought) significantly affected participants' reactions. Images of forest fires, as opposed to images of melting ice or extreme drought, generated the strongest reactions from participants. All people have experienced fire—both the helpful and destructive aspects—and this level of familiarity may make the images more effective. In addition, the effects from forest fires, and other types of fires, are more acute (as opposed to chronic), as well as immediate and devastating than drought and melting ice.

The prevalence of highly damaging fires has increased over the past several years, not only in the Western U.S. but more importantly in areas such as the Southeast United States where wildfires have been less prevalent (Westerling, Hidalgo, Cayan, & Swetnam, 2006). Even though this increase in wildfires has occurred over time and due to conditions the general public cannot easily perceive, the fires themselves are highly visible when they occur and attract significant attention in the media, making wildfires are more 'top of mind' for people than ever before. As a result, it is possible that images of fire can open the door to educating people about climate change.

The relationship of wildfire to climate change encompasses several different issues. Wildfires ignite from either a human cause (e.g. a campfire left burning) or a natural cause (e.g. a lightning strike). While human activities can influence an increase in the likelihood of wildfires, scientists have noticed that areas that are protected from human activities have seen an increase in fires, leading scientists to believe that climate change is a major factor (Chinura et al., 2011). The warming climate causes snow to melt earlier in the spring, thus soil dries out earlier and is dry for a longer period of time, providing more fuel for any fires that ignite (Westerling et al., 2006). Government fire suppression programs have also allowed for the proliferation of trees that are less fire-tolerant, which combined with the dry soil creates wildfires are more intense and long burning (Pechony & Shindel, 2010). The wildfire season is also lengthening. Wildfires now are occurring in a much broader time frame as opposed to during a specific summer period—some scientists argue that in the Southwest, fire season will extend year-round rather than several months in a year (Pechony & Shindell, 2010).

There is also a connection between increased wildfires and flash floods. Wildfires destroy plants that help keep soil in place and soak up excess water from an area. Thus, when rains come, the risk of flash floods will increase. Wildfires threaten people through damage to life and property particularly at the urban/forest interface and increase local air pollution, causing breathing difficulties even in healthy individuals. As a result, increases in wildfires can affect people who never even venture out into the woods. Connecting the effects of wildfires to larger climate change issues may be the tipping point to increase the salience of climate change for them. Future research should examine whether specific elements of fire imagery—in particular, the international/domestic location of the fire, and the presence or absence of people—can increase engagement with fire imagery to affect salience and subsequent behaviors related to the climate among people who see the image.

The findings of this study add to the theoretical understanding of the effects of images regarding emotional reaction and engagement. The study findings also provide a direction for future research, as well as news media coverage and public communication campaigns. In addition, the study confirmed *New York Times'* photojournalist Josh Haner's idea that the right images that create emotional connection and engagement. This can affect audience perceptions of the seriousness of climate change to a greater degree than the stereotypical climate images used on a regular basis (personal communication, May 5, 2016). These results suggest it is possible for certain imagery to affect emotions and engagement, and thus perhaps raise the salience of climate change among audiences.

References

Adam, P. S., Quinn, S., & Edmonds, R. (2007). *Eyetracking the news: A story of print and online reading.* St. Petersburg, FL: The Poynter Institute.

Bas, O., & Grabe, M. E. (2015). Emotion-provoking personalization of news: Informing citizens and closing the knowledge gap? *Communication Research, 42*(2), 159-185. DOI: 10.1177/0093650213514602

Casebeer, A. L., & Verhoef, M. J. (1997). Combining qualitative and quantitative research methods: Considering the possibilities for enhancing the study of chronic diseases. *Chronic Diseases and Injuries in Canada, 18*(3), 130.

Chmura, D. J., Anderson, P. D., Howe, G. T., Harrington, C. A., Halofsky, J. E., Peterson, D. L., Shaw, D. & Clair, J. B. S. (2011). Forest responses to climate change in the northwestern United States: Ecophysiological foundations for adaptive management. *Forest Ecology and Management, 261*(7), 1121-1142. DOI: 10.1016/j.foreco.2010.12.040

DeVellis, R. F. (2012). *Scale development: Theory and applications.* Los Angeles, CA: Sage.

Ewbank, M. P., Barnard, P. J., Croucher, C. J., Ramponi, C., & Calder, A. J. (2009). The amygdala response to images with impact. *Social Cognitive and Affective Neuroscience, 4*(2), 127-133. DOI: 10.1093/scan/nsn048

Gallup (2016). Most important problems. Retrieved from http://www.gallup.com/poll/1675/most-important-problem.aspx

Garcia, M. (2002). *Pure design.* St. Petersburg, FL: Miller Media.

Griffin, M. (1999). The great war photographs: Constructing myths of history and photojournalism. In Bonnie Brennen and Hanno Hardt (Eds.), *Picturing the past: Media, history, and photography* (pp. 122-157). University of Illinois Press.

Hansen, A., & Machin, D. (2008). Visually branding the environment: Climate change as a marketing opportunity. *Discourse Studies, 10*(6), 777-794. DOI: 10.1177/1461445608098200

Hart, P. S., & Feldman, L. (2016). The impact of climate change-related imagery and text on public opinion and behavior change. *Science Communication, 38*(4), 415-441. DOI: 10.1177/1075547016655357

King, C., & Lester, P. (2005). Photographic coverage during the Persian Gulf and Iraqi wars in three U.S. newspapers. *Journalism & Mass Communication Quarterly, 82*(3), 623-637. DOI: 10.1177/107769900508200309

Kumar, D. (2006). Media, war, and propaganda: Strategies of information management during the 2003 Iraq war. *Communication and Critical/Cultural Studies, 3*(1), 48-69. DOI: 10.1080/14791420500505650

Leiserowitz, A. (2007). Communicating the risks of global warming: American risk perceptions, affective images, and interpretive communities. *Creating a climate for change: Communicating climate change and facilitating social change,* 44-63. http://dx.doi.org/10.1017/CBO9780511535871.005

Lester, P. M. (2005). *Visual communication: images with messages* (4th ed.). Belmont, CA: Thomson Wadsworth.

Lippmann, W. (1922). *Public opinion.* New York: Free Press.

Louw, P. E. (2003). The war against terrorism' a public relations challenge for the Pentagon. *Gazette, 65*(3), 211-230. DOI: 10.1177/0016549203065003001

Maier, S. R., Slovic, P., & Mayorga, M. (2016). Reader reaction to news of mass suffering: Assessing the influence of story form and emotional response. *Journalism, 18*(8), 1011-1029. doi 1464884916663597

McIntyre, K., & Sobel, M. (2017). Motivating news audiences: Shock them or provide them with solutions? *Comunicación y Sociedad, 30*(1), 39. DOI: 10.15581/003.30.1.39-56

Moeller, S. D. (1999). *Compassion fatigue: How the media sell disease, famine, war and death.* New York: Routledge.

Myrick, J. G., & Evans, S. D. (2014). Do PSAs take a bite out of Shark Week? The effects of juxtaposing environmental messages with violent images of shark attacks. *Science Communication, 36*(5), 544-569. DOI: 10.1177/1075547014547159

NASA. (2017). The consequences of climate change. Retrieved from https://climate.nasa.gov/effects/

Oliver, M. B., Dillard, J. P., Bae, K., & Tamul, D. J. (2012). The effect of narrative news format on empathy for stigmatized groups. *Journalism & Mass Communication Quarterly, 89*(2), 205-224. DOI: 10.1177/1077699012439020

O'Neill, S. J. (2013). Image matters: Climate change imagery in US, UK and Australian newspapers. *Geoforum, 49,* 10-19. DOI: 10.1016/j.geoforum.2013.04.030

O'Neill, S., & Nicholson-Cole, S. (2009). "Fear won't do it" promoting positive engagement with climate change through visual and iconic representations. *Science Communication, 30*(3), 355-379. DOI: 10.1177/1075547008329201

O'Neill, S. J., & Smith, N. (2014). Climate change and visual imagery. *Wiley Interdisciplinary Reviews: Climate Change, 5*(1), 73-87. DOI: 10.1002/wcc.249

Paivio, A., Rogers, T. B., & Smythe, P. C. (1968). Why are pictures easier to recall than words? *Psychonomic Science, 11*(4), 137-138. DOI: 10.3758/BF03331011

Pechony, O., & Shindell, D. T. (2010). Driving forces of global wildfires over the past millennium and the forthcoming century. *Proceedings of the National Academy of Sciences, 107*(45), 19167-19170. DOI: 10.1073/pnas.1003669107

Prisco, J. (2016, November 18). This is what climate change looks like. CNN. Retrieved from http://www.cnn.com/2016/11/16/world/cop22-photo-award/

Roser-Renouf, C., Maibach, E., Leiserowitz, A., & Rosenthal, S. (2016). *Global warming's six Americas and the election, 2016.* Yale University and George Mason University. New Haven, CT: Yale Program on Climate Change Communication.

van der Linden, S., Leiserowitz, A., Rosenthal, S., & Maibach, E. (2017). Inoculating the public against misinformation about climate change. *Global Challenges, 1*(2), 1600008. doi 10.1002/gch2.201600008

Västfjäll, D., Slovic, P., Mayorga, M., & Peters, E. (2014). Compassion fade: Affect and charity are greatest for a single child in need. *PloS one, 9*(6), e100115. DOI: 10.1371/journal.pone.0100115

Westerling, A. L., Hidalgo, H. G., Cayan, D. R., & Swetnam, T. W. (2006). Warming and earlier spring increase western US forest wildfire activity. *Science, 313*(5789), 940-943. DOI: 10.1126/science.1128834

Chapter 5

Arcane and Hidden:
Why the State Public Utilities
Commissions are so Difficult for Climate
Change Communications

Nancy LaPlaca, J.D.

Introduction

It's probably true that there is no more boring word for most Americans than "regulatory." For most people, it makes your head hurt. But understanding state-level utility regulatory decisions is important for people who are concerned about climate change because these public utilities commissions are the folks who are deciding right now whether our future will be fueled by clean energy or yet more fossil fuels.

State level authority over electric power plants

Authority over electric utilities is generally at the state—not federal—level, with some notable exceptions (The Regulatory Assistance Project, 2011). The federal government does play a role in regulating power plants and can directly affect the cost of electricity in every state, for example, by adding a carbon fee. But permission to build the power plant, most of the permitting processes, and the authority to allow a utility to collect money from customers to pay for power plants, is at the state level. (This essay won't address regulated versus deregulated states, or nuclear power plants, which complicate the matter because federal regulators play a larger role.)

State regulators (and sometimes legislators) in each state often determine the state's electricity mix, i.e. how much coal, natural gas, nuclear, solar, wind, energy efficiency and other resources are used to generate (or save) electricity for the state (The Regulatory Assistance Project, 2011). They typically do this through state agencies called public utility commissions (PUCs). While each state is unique, there are broad general principles about state public utility commissions.

Some state regulators are appointed, a few are elected; quasi-judicial agencies

Of the fifty U.S. states, about a dozen are elected, while the rest are appointed (The Regulatory Assistance Project, 2011). In some states, such as Arizona, the PUC is its own branch of government, with a very high degree of independence (Arizona Corporation Commission, n.d.).

To further confuse the matter, about seven states have constitutional commissions, which means that the PUC has a lot more power to set policy (The Regulatory Assistance Project, 2011). The rest of the states are statutory, which means that the legislature and governor determine policies such as whether to implement renewable energy portfolios or energy efficiency goals. Thus, in a constitutional state, the PUC makes these decisions on its own, while in a statutory state, renewable portfolio standards or energy efficiency goals must become law before the PUC can implement them.

For example, Arizona, which is a constitutional state, gives its five elected commissioners complete authority to set electricity policy (as well as natural gas, and some water and securities policies). This means that the state legislature and governor have no authority to change or modify decisions made by the five commissioners.

As quasi-judicial agencies, PUCs are steeped in the vagaries of administrative law. Thus, it's difficult for a reviewing court to change a PUC decision because courts give these agencies a high level of *deference*. This deference is given because PUCs have a lot of expertise in a very complex area of law, so its decisions must be very obviously bad to be reconsidered or overturned by a reviewing court (The Regulatory Assistance Project, 2011). On a practical level, this means that it's harder for clean energy advocates to successfully challenge a PUC decision.

Because PUCs have such specialized knowledge, and often have uniquely qualified judges and attorneys working on these issues, decisions tend to be final and are very difficult to overturn.

Everything about state PUCs is legally arcane and complex: the language, the principles, the process, and the players. The high level of complexity of PUCs, and the fact that policies are created in each state, makes it difficult for people working on climate change by promoting policies that allow clean energy to thrive.

It's not rocket science, it's the same old pay-to-play

Additionally, electric utilities are usually the most politically powerful players in any given state. In states with elected PUCs, utilities spend vast sums to elect "friendly" regulators (Roberts, 2017b). *Follow the Money*, a project of the nonpartisan National Institute on Money in State Politics, which gathers information about campaign contributions and political lobbying, reports that industries spent $51 million over an 8-year period in 12 states with elected regulators (Burgam, 2015). Most of the money comes from the industries being regulated by the PUCs. In states with appointed regulators, utilities spend vast sums on gubernatorial races so that they can influence PUC appointments made by the governor (Heald, 2017).

As an example, consider the state of Arizona. Over the past few years, Arizona's PUC (called the Corporation Commission) has been particularly noteworthy. The sunny state of AZ has an energy mix of about 5% solar and 40% coal (U.S. Energy Information Administration, 2016b). In July 2017, former AZ Commission Chair Gary Pierce was indicted for fraud and bribery, i.e. vote-selling, along with (now former) Arizona Public Service Company lobbyist Jim Norton (Roberts, 2017a). The indictment states that Commissioner Pierce voted for a rate increase in exchange for $31,000 in cash and ownership in a $350,000 piece of property. APS is notorious for its role in Arizona elections and played a role in raising $750,000 for Commissioner Pierce's son, Justin, during his 2014 campaign for Arizona Secretary of State (Roberts, 2014).

In early 2016, then-Chair Susan Bitter-Smith was forced to resign due to conflicts of interest. Along with her $80,000 per year taxpayer-paid salary, she was raking in over $200,000 per year to consult with the very industries she was regulating (Roberts, 2015). Commissioner Bitter-Smith resigned before the case went to the state Supreme Court.

Commissioner Bob Stump exchanged thousands of text messages with utility executives, dark money groups, candidates and other parties on a state-provided cell phone, but was able to keep the messages secret, even after he initially "lost" the phone (which he later "found") (Roberts, 2016).

The bound-to-fail saga of "clean" coal has cost ratepayers dearly, as companies like Duke Energy dealt with scandals at the Indiana PUC that cost both top-level utility executives and commissioners their jobs (Citizens Action Coalition, 2012). A recent lawsuit filed by an engineer alleges that top-level utility executives knew since 2012 that its now-$7.5 billion "clean" coal plant would be far more expensive to run than the models they used (Kelly, 2017).

Despite these obvious bad decisions and cronyism, utility executives are very highly paid: Lynn Good at Duke Energy's salary is about $14 million per year (Henderson, 2017), Southern Company's Tom Fanning got a raise to $16 million this past year (Grantham, 2017), despite the failed "clean" coal plant and a very expensive nuclear boondoggle. APS CEO Don Brandt, despite the fact that he's helping to kill solar in one of the sunniest regions in the world, is paid $50,000 per day (Wiles, 2016).

It's complicated

In a nutshell, PUCs are complicated. What's even more complex are the processes by which decisions are made at the PUCs. The terminology alone will keep you busy for a year, and then learning the different types of dockets (i.e., cases) such as rate cases (which set what customers pay, and how much profit a utility can make), or integrated resource plans (where a utility tells the world what kinds of power plants it plans to build in the next ten to fifteen years), or renewable portfolio standards (in the 30 or so states that actually have renewable energy goals), or fuel dockets (where utilities discuss how much fuel they plan to purchase)—the list is long.

How does one communicate these issues? How does one make general statements about a process with exceptions, each more complex than the rule? It's very difficult to do so in a way that's understandable for most citizens, particularly given that many don't see the relevance of these entities to their daily lives.

This complexity is why it's been so easy for PUCs to be under the radar despite their significant influence over energy policy—and by extent, climate policy. This complexity is why Florida, the Sunshine State, has less than 0.5% solar (U.S. Energy Information Administration, 2016a). Or why Arizonans are paying $38 million more per year for electricity from one of the Western U.S.'s dirtiest, oldest coal plants rather than purchasing power on the open market, despite clear evidence that solar is far cheaper over its lifetime (Randazzo, 2017).

Some of the sunniest states in the U.S. have the least amount of solar: New Mexico 3.4%, Utah 3.56%, Colorado 2%, Arizona 5%, Texas 0.29%, Montana 0.04%, Idaho 0.61%, Florida 0.31% (Solar Energy Industries of America, 2017).

Why? Commissioners have the power to vote, and those votes tend to be final. Arizona regulators decided that coal is better than solar (LaPlaca, 2017). Florida regulators add thousands of megawatts (MWs) of new natural gas power plants and pipelines in the Sunshine State, which currently spends $8 billion per year importing coal and natural gas (U.S. Energy Information Administration, 2015).

The other reason is that the rules regulators follow are way behind the times. For example, the fact that health and environmental damages from coal-fired electricity are between 17 and 27 cents per kilowatt-hour (kWh) (Romm, 2011) is information that simply isn't considered or even acknowledged by most regulators. In the same vein, the fact that clean energy uses very little water and creates no pollution has no "value" in the current regulatory regime in the vast majority of states.

This is where real change in terms of the climate and environment can happen: outdated rules no longer fit our new paradigm of clean, locally-sited and locally-owned energy. We know what to do, we just need to get regulators and utilities to act in our interests, and not the interests of the coal, natural gas, pipeline and other fossil fuel companies.

Where do we go from here?

Environmental interveners and policy experts at state PUCs need climate communications help. Arcane policies and decisions that help utilities rather than customers need to be called out, but without solid communications plans, it is difficult for environmental groups and experts to do so.

We're getting there. In Nevada, residents might not have understood all the details of why solar was killed (the rate paid for solar fed into the grid was drastically reduced, from 11.6 cents per kWh to 5.5 cents/kWh when fully implemented (Pyper, 2015), but they knew that solar companies closed shop and moved out in droves (Walton, 2017). The backlash was so large that the PUC's decision to make rooftop solar uneconomical was completely reversed two years later. However, the battle continues, as NV Energy continues to push against rooftop solar.

In Arizona, hundreds show up for hearings to lament the assault on solar, on energy efficiency, and on good policy. But while solar is getting hammered in Arizona, and residents spend $2 to $3 billion per year importing coal and natural gas (U.S. Energy Information Administration, n.d.), regulators get away with being elected essentially with utility funds (Roberts, 2017a).

Difficult as the push has been for clean energy, organizers have had lots of success in the many bad decisions have been stopped (EQ Research, n.d.). Across the U.S., from California to North Carolina, organizers have used social media, intervened in dockets, showed up for hearings, and made their voices heard. In state after state, activists clearly understand and articulate the value clean energy brings.

It's time to occupy the PUCs

As an example of how communications can help bolster efforts to influence PUCs, consider BOLD Nebraska, a citizens' organization working on issues of land and water safety and climate change has made a dent at the normally impenetrable PUC. They're on to something: they've asked landowners in the path of the Keystone Pipeline—a proposed pipeline transporting tar sands from Canada across the Great Plains—to participate in the permitting process at the state utilities board by showing up at hearings and submitting comments. Nearly a half million comments denouncing Keystone were filed, describing the risk the pipeline presents (Hefflinger, 2017). BOLD Nebraska's plan to add citizen input to a process that is usually reserved to insiders, utility lawyers and a handful of environmental attorneys was a resounding success. People showed up and demanded that their voices be heard (Hefflinger, 2017).

What do climate activists and concerned citizens need to do at the PUCs? As usual, sunshine is the best disinfectant. We need to make sure regulators like those in Arizona explain why they think coal should be supported, and not solar. Or ask Florida's Commission why they want to invest billions of ratepayer funds in natural gas pipelines and power plants rather than solar or energy efficiency.

Communications strategies that take into consideration the complexity of PUCs and their relative obscurity for most of the public are essential to getting this message out. Let's go.

References

Arizona Corporation Commission. (n.d.). Arizona Corporation Commission. Retrieved from http://www.azcc.gov/

Burgam, C. (2015, May 18). $51 Million: Elected utility regulators score big bucks. Retrieved from https://www.followthemoney.org/research/blog/51-million-elected-utility-regulators-score-big-bucks/

Citizens Action Coalition. (2012, December 18). IURC: Impervious to ethics scandal. Retrieved from http://www.citact.org/energy-policy-fossil-fuels-and-nuclear-energy-utility-rates-and-regulation-issues-utility-duke/duk-0

EQ Research. (n.d.). Policy research & analysis for the Clean Energy Sector. Retrieved from https://eq-research.com/

Grantham, R. (2017, April 3). Southern chief's pay package rises to $15.8M. *The Atlanta Journal-Constitution*. Retrieved from http://www.myajc.com/business/southern-chief-pay-package-rises/N8iJwqiDpyeYn4GjY5Rb8J/

Heald, S. (2017, May 30). UVA Prof. Vivian Thomson's "Climate of Capitulation" is essential reading in this election year. Retrieved from https://powerforthepeopleva.com/2017/05/30/uva-prof-vivian-thomsons-climate-of-capitulation-is-essential-reading-in-this-election-year/

Hefflinger, M. (2017, August 15). Recap: Keystone XL Intervenor Hearings at the PSC. Retrieved from http://boldnebraska.org/recap-keystone-xl-intervenor-hearings-at-the-psc/

Henderson, B. (2017, March 3). Duke Energy CEO's pay jumped 27 percent to $13.8 million last year. *The Charlotte Observer*. Retrieved from http://www.charlotteobserver.com/news/local/article136276868.html

Kelly, S. (2017, August 8). New fraud allegations emerge at troubled "clean coal" project as Southern Co. records multi-billion loss. Retrieved August from https://www.desmogblog.com/2017/08/08/southern-company-fraud-allegations-kemper-clean-coal-project

LaPlaca, N. (2017). Andy Tobin pushes to keep open dirtiest coal plant in the Western United States. Retrieved from http://www.energyandpolicy.org/andy-tobin-coal-navajo-generating-station/

Pyper, J. (2015, December 23). Nevada regulators eliminate retail rate net metering for new and existing solar customers. Retrieved from https://www.greentechmedia.com/articles/read/nevada-regulators-eliminate-retail-rate-net-metering-for-new-and-existing-s

Randazzo, R. (2017, May 22). 10 challenges to keeping the Navajo Generating Station open. *The Arizona Republic*. Retrieved from http://www.azcentral.com/story/money/business/energy/2017/05/22/arizona-10-challenges-keeping-navajo-generating-station-open/332911001/

Roberts, L. (2014, July 3). Who is it that so badly wants Justin Pierce elected SOS? *The Arizona Republic*. Retrieved from http://www.azcentral.com/story/laurieroberts/2014/07/03/justin-pierce-dark-money-secretary-of-state/12149775/

Roberts, L. (2015, September 14). Roberts: Susan Bitter Smith should resign. *The Arizona Republic*. Retrieved from http://www.azcentral.com/story/opinion/op-ed/laurieroberts/2015/09/14/susan-bitter-smith-should-resign-arizona-corporation-commission/72265662/

Roberts, L. (2016, May 31). Roberts: Bob Stump's texts to remain forever a mystery. *The Arizona Republic*. Retrieved from http://www.azcentral.com/story/opinion/op-ed/laurieroberts/2016/05/31/roberts-bob-stumps-texts-remain-forever-mystery/85215512/

Roberts, L. (2017a, May 30). Roberts: More to come in Corporation Commission scandal? *The Arizona Republic*. Retrieved from http://www.azcentral.com/story/opinion/op-ed/laurieroberts/2017/05/30/roberts-more-come-corporation-commission-scandal/356294001/

Roberts, L. (2017b, August 7). Can Arizona's utility regulators look any worse? (Why, yes, they can). *The Arizona Republic*. Retrieved from http://www.azcentral.com/story/opinion/op-ed/laurieroberts/2017/08/07/can-arizonas-utility-regulators-look-any-worse-why-yes-they-can/547097001/

Romm, J. (2011, February 16). Life-cycle study: Accounting for total harm from coal would add "close to 17.8¢/kWh of electricity generated." Retrieved from https://thinkprogress.org/life-cycle-study-accounting-for-total-harm-from-coal-would-add-close-to-17-8-kwh-of-electricity-6e2ca8efc44a/

Solar Energy Industries of America. (2017). State Solar Policy. Retrieved from http://www.seia.org/policy/state-solar-policy

The Regulatory Assistance Project. (2011). *Electricity regulation In the US: A guide.* Montpelier, VT: The Regulatory Assistance Project. Retrieved from http://www.raponline.org/wp-content/uploads/2016/05/rap-lazar-electricityregulationintheus-guide-2011-03.pdf

U.S. Energy Information Administration. (2016a, August 18). Florida - State energy profile overview. Retrieved August 24, 2017, from https://www.eia.gov/state/?sid=FL

U.S. Energy Information Administration. (2016b, December 15). Arizona - State energy profile overview. Retrieved from https://www.eia.gov/state/?sid=AZ

U.S. Energy Information Administration. (2015). Electric power sector energy Expenditure estimates, 2015 (Million Dollars). Retrieved from https://www.eia.gov/state/seds/data.php?incfile=/state/seds/sep_sum/html/sum_ex_eu.html&sid=US

Walton, R. (2017, June 1). Resurrecting retail rate net metering could cost $1.3B, NV Energy warns. Retrieved from http://www.utilitydive.com/news/resurrecting-retail-rate-net-metering-could-could-cost-13b-nv-energy-war/443976/

Wiles, R. (2016, June 3). Profits pave way to record CEO pay in Arizona. *The Arizona Republic.* Retrieved from http://www.azcentral.com/story/money/business/jobs/2016/06/03/profits-pave-way-record-ceo-pay-arizona/85202696/

Chapter 6

Reframing the Narrative Around Solar Technology: Unlikely Opportunities for Bipartisanship in an Increasingly Divided Nation

Ishana Ratan

Introduction

"I want tariffs. Bring me some tariffs!" (Levin, 2017, par 4) declared President Donald Trump during one of his recurring outbursts against foreign firms in the manufacturing sector and their low-cost imports, which the current Administration claims are flooding the United States market. *Mr. President, we will give you some tariffs. We have your tariffs!* responded the domestic manufacturing sector, looking to translate Trump's protectionist pontificating into real trade policy. Trump's economic aspirations are centered around protecting domestic manufacturing jobs by erecting trade barriers against China, the primary trade rival of the United States (Rosenfeld, 2017). This trade policy was popularized during the past election cycle after years of consensus regarding free trade and lends a voice to the increasing economic anxieties of blue-collar manufacturing workers in America and the struggling industries that employ them. Furthermore, Trump has taken a strong stance against environmental protection, as evidenced by his refutation of the Paris Agreement (Meyer, 2017) and dogmatic denial of climate change in the wake of massive climate-related natural disasters (Inslee, 2017). One industry lies directly in the crosshairs of Trump's fervent call for increased economic protectionism and simultaneous ignorance towards environmental degradation: solar power.

From 2008 to 2013, the global solar market rapidly expanded from a capacity of 15,844 megawatts per year to 368,000 in 2017 as Chinese solar cell production capacity and exports dramatically increased. Chinese companies executed an industrial coup d'etat, capturing unprecedented shares of the global crystalline polysilicon photovoltaic cell (CSPV) manufacturing market. During this time, China's expansion facilitated the price of solar cells' decline by 80 percent, catapulting residential solar panels to new levels of affordability and heralding a new chapter in the future of green energy. Public opinion on solar expansion is also overwhelmingly positive; 89 percent of Americans support solar expansion, and residential solar has become increasingly popular due to its newfound affordability (Kennedy, 2016). However, Trump's attachment to the manufacturing sector and lambasting of Chinese imports indicates that the current administration will seek to pursue a protectionist policy in the near future. Further trade barriers are capable of destabilizing solar's growth and sparking a trade war with China (Dana, 2017), to the benefit of United States producers struggling to turn a profit or maintain market share in an increasingly competitive world market (Hill, 2017). The most recent case litigated at the International Trade Commission will preempt pollution to the tune of 7 million metric tons CO_2 equivalent per year by 2030 and 19 million metric tons annually by 2050 (Page, 2017). However, key segments of the public are vulnerable to misleading narratives structured by conservative elites, while potential activists remain unengaged due to unfocused messaging from pro-trade and pro-solar organizations. Framing theory points to potential strategies in engaging disillusioned voters in the climate change debate and countering the manufacturing sectors' narrative via communication strategies resonant with target audiences.

During the 2008 recession, China's surge in production and drop in solar panel prices came at the expense of less efficient United States firms, many of which had limited access to low-interest loans and were not effectively subsidized (Ball, Reicher, Sun, & Pollock, 2017). American producers spin their decreasing global market share as a byproduct of Chinese expansion and cost-cutting via cheap labor inputs rather than domestic inefficiency. Petitioners in litigation against Chinese exporters argue that claims that U.S. producers are injured because the U.S. manufacturing industry, which initially pioneered photovoltaics technology, has failed to compete with its global competitors in terms of efficiency and product offerings are false. However, research from National Renewable Energy Laboratory has determined that China's true cost advantage stems not from cheap labor, but from vertically integrated supply chains and internal economies of scale, which allow the largest firms to produce most efficiently, along multiple phases of the supply chains (Goodrich, Powell, James, Woodhouse, & Buonassisi, 2013). This type of market structure lends itself to a highly concentrated industry with a few large producers, as opposed to a large number of small firms with constant returns to scale.

SolarWorld argues that Chinese competition has driven the number of United States manufacturing firms from over thirty in 2012 to two in 2017 through supplying an overcapacity of solar cells in the global market. However, while overcapacity has resulted in a steep decline in price and industrial consolidation has driven small scale competitors out of the market, neither are evidence of unfair trade practices. Solar is a technology-intensive industry, which lends itself to an imperfectly competitive market structure, economies of scale, and increasingly concentrated firms (Varian, 2001). Domestic producers blame the decline of the profitability of manufacturing on cost competition, without examining the larger market forces at play. Furthermore, U.S. manufacturers fail to note that in 2013, after the implementation of the first round of countervailing and antidumping duties, over 300 Chinese solar firms exited the market (Osborne, 2013), indicating that the effects of overcapacity not only shuttered smaller United States solar manufacturers but caused domestic level Chinese producers, incapable of exporting or heavily investing in research in development, to similarly close. These tariffs simply increased incentives for competitive firm strategy, and only shuttered firms unable to step up to the challenge. Empirical evidence shows that the solar cell production industry favors internal economies of scale, where costs decrease the more units produced, and smaller firms struggle to compete and survive in the global economy, regardless of the country in which the industry is concentrated. (Powell, et al., 2015) Although domestic firms may have pioneered large scale manufacturing of CSPV technology, Chinese supply chains and an increasingly efficient business model has rendered United States solar cell manufacturing an industry past its heyday, with little potential for future growth regardless of protectionist policy.

However, despite Chinese competition in the manufacturing sector, market analysis suggests that the United States solar market is not truly contracting, despite the narrative of producers. According to the market analysis, the domestic market share of U.S. producers fell from 21.0 percent in 2012 to 11.0 percent in 2016, despite $4 billion growth of the U.S. market over the same period (Miles, 2017). This indicates that while domestic manufacturing has experienced a downturn in the last decade, certain segments of the domestic industry have indeed been growing, and successfully competing in the market. Inside the United States solar market exist two opposite segments of the supply chain, manufacturing and installation. While the former has experienced declining profit margins and market loss with the advent of Chinese production, the latter has grown significantly with the increasingly affordable cost of residential solar. Manufacturing represents an upstream segment of the solar market, producing the physical goods necessary to assemble complete panels, which are then assembled, and distributed for sale. At the downstream segment of the supply chain lies the installation industry, a service driven sector that encompasses a variety of products (Solar Energy Industry Association, 2014). Installation inherently has higher barriers to market entry, as it requires skilled labor, and is attractive to prospective investors due to the variety of services it encompasses, including system monitoring, inverter installation, and project financing (Solar Panel Installation, 2017). The domestic solar industry is split between these two segments -- a problematic scenario for constructing cohesive solar policy to the benefit of American consumers.

United States manufacturers of CSPV cells argue that they provide an essential service to the solar industry, employ significant portions of the US Solar industry, and account for a large segment of the value added in the solar panel production supply chain. However, jobs in manufacturing have remained stable at roughly 35,000 employees, or 20 percent of domestic solar workers, since 2012 -- despite multiple rounds of tariffs aimed at restricting foreign producers' share of the U.S. market. Conversely, the installation industry has grown from 40,000 workers in 2011 to over 137,000 in 2016 (National Solar Jobs Census, 2016). Manufacturing also represents a comparatively low percentage of value added along the panel production supply chain, while other segments, primarily research, development and installation, add considerably more value to the final product and are better suited to provide Americans with skilled employment opportunities. Excluding the cost of raw materials themselves, services in solar installation can account for upwards of 60 percent value added -- and the United States has a flourishing installation industry that has shown consistent growth in tandem with the expansion of low-cost residential solar. (Zhao, 2015)

However, the installation industry's growth and development are at stake in the newest round of antidumping and countervailing duty investigations applying to CSPV producers from 163 countries. Unbiased research has predicted that in the worst-case scenario, panel prices may double (Ryan & Dlouhy, 2017). Over 88,000 jobs in the burgeoning installation industry could be lost to decline in demand, while in an economy uninhibited by trade barriers, the market is on track to double residential photovoltaic deployment by 2019 and triple by 2021 (Reuter & Kuebler, 2017). If these duties were to be imposed, the domestic installation industry would be drastically damaged, as returns on investment falter and consumers are unable to enter the residential solar market (Marshall, Storrow, Reilly, & Northey, 2017). This results in stymied solar deployment-- which ultimately increases carbon output and contributes to even greater environmental degradation. Furthermore, if the Solar 201 case were to be implemented, industry growth could be stymied by 66 percent (Ryan, 2017). Ultimately, affordable imported solar panels are equivalent with expansion in domestic utilization of green energy, and growth in an industry with high levels of value added in the production supply chain.

Framing theory and the manufacturing narrative

Framing refers to the presentation of an issue in the media, and deliberate inclusions and exclusion of attributes of the narrative to create a certain public response (Scheufele & Tewksbury, 2007). An issue may be framed in different ways by various organizations in an attempt to garner support from a particular audience, by appealing to either or both their moral values or rational decision-making capabilities. Existing literature has examined the effects of framing in determining the lens through which the population views issues (Snow, Burke, Wordon, & Benford, 1986). Communication strategies may either utilize "ethical" or "material" frame while interpreting an issue, and the method of framing employed affects the audience's response to not only the issue at hand but other situations they face in the future. Ethical frames activate values, beliefs, and morals in the decision-making process, and are linked to an individual's sense of personal identity. Material frames, on the other hand, involve rational, cost-benefit decisions unrelated to one's sense of self (Abramson & Inglehart, 1995). Previous research has indicated that an individual first exposed and influenced by ethical frames has a high probability of using ethical judgement in future determinations regarding related issues (Nelson & Wiley, 2001).

However, there is a great difference between ethical determinations and rational determinations, primarily regarding their mutability. Nelson and Wiley (2001) suggest that because ethical frames are tied to an individual's self-perception, they are less subject to cost-benefit analysis than material frames. The former is a non-compensatory frame; positives cannot offset negatives and results in an inflexible position founded on a select few issues. Compensatory frames, in contrast, are subject to cost-benefit analysis and are prone to change with an individual's objective self-interest (Nelson & Wiley, 2001). In the case of solar energy, the manufacturing sector's argument has often been couched in personal anecdotes that speak to the individual's sense of loss and economic strife, while pro-trade and pro-solar policy has been portrayed at best through empirical analysis, and at worst as an elitist, out-of-touch stance that fails to resonate with the needs of working-class Americans. Framing analysis provides a theoretical framework to analyze the complex narratives surrounding international trade policy, manufacturing, and climate change. The present framing of this issue, particularly within the current political climate, creates a false dichotomy that fails to resolve the issues regarding trade policy and solar power. Media coverage of trade policy further agitates the "us vs. them" mentality of mercantilism, only setting American production back while foreign production continues to rise. Ultimately, the debate regarding solar reflects the divergence in narratives between the manufacturing sector and the interests of the general public and the capabilities of framing in affecting how the population perceives an issue.

While statistical measures of the general public's support for solar remains strong, diverging narratives of the same scenario fight for public opinion and media distribution. Meanwhile, the contention between international solar manufacturers and the domestic intra-industry rift between producers and installers threatens to upend the industry. Research suggests that the loss of market share for American solar manufacturers is more complex than the "Chinese stealing jobs," but producers' messaging and Trump's unshakable support for "Factory America" paints a poignant narrative of suffering solar production and unemployed blue-collar workers (Weingarten, 2016). Trump's narrative highlights the ethical and moral reprehensibility of supporting globalization and outsourcing, in the grounds that it inhibits jobs that Americans both economically and ethically deserve. Existing research classifies this type of narrative as employing "ethical" framing, as it uses language that taps into the recipient's core values and sense of self-identity (Nelson & Wiley, 2001). Consequently, the personal, poignant narrative of unemployed blue-collar workers creates non-compensatory judgement that ties trade policy to the traditional values and livelihood of rural America. Both the manufacturing sector and Trump portray free trade in photovoltaics and American jobs as a zero-sum game and insinuate that those who do not support such a narrative are un-American and are inhibiting blue-collar workers from earning a sustainable living.

The manufacturing sector's narrative, focused on cheap Chinese exports' responsibility for traumatic domestic injury and job loss, gained traction as domestic firms promoted their case in the media and courtrooms by using pathos heavy language that resonated with those most hurt by trade and globalization (Greenhouse, 2016). In general, American manufacturing experienced a significant decline in output in the wake of Chinese capacity expansion, vertical integration of supply chains, and increased automation, and it has been in the self-interest of domestic firms to collect information regarding their plight and create a cohesive narrative portraying the manufacturing sector in a sympathetic light (Matsuyama, 2009). Empirical evidence indicates that Chinese expansion was not based on cost competition intended to edge domestic firms out of the market (Atkinson, Steward, Andes, & Ezell, 2012), yet firms including SolarWorld and Suniva portray themselves victims held hostage by Chinese producers and foreign government subsidies. (Goodrich et al. 2013). Conversely, organizations such as the Solar Energy Industry Association (SEIA), a coalition of multiple small domestic firms at varying stages of the supply chain, from research and development to installation, have been typically non-confrontational regarding periodic raises in trade barriers. However, industry stability has been newly threatened by the impending determination of injury against domestic manufacturing firms by the International Trade Commission, and the following proposed remedy of increased protection against imported panels. This case would levy duties on 163 countries, some of which have trade agreements with the United States, in an unprecedented regression of trade policy hearkening back to the 2002 Bush moratorium on foreign steel (Solar Section 201 Trade Case, 2017). Meanwhile, consumers of solar panels have not attempted any method of collective action to continue benefiting from affordable renewable energy, which is threatened by the potential increase in the price of residential solar panels following the new case.

Framing theory provides an explanation for the success of the manufacturing sector in developing an unwavering, invested support base, while analysis of firm-level collective action dilemmas provide a framework to view the abilities and incentives of manufacturing firms to act as key providers of information for the government, media, and general public. Furthermore, collective action theory also underscores the structural barriers opposing consumer driven engagement and action. Olson's Logic of Collective Action posits that firm involvement in the political process is greater in heavily concentrated industries (Sufrin & Olson, 1966), and this theory highlights the ability of domestic solar manufacturers, namely Suniva and SolarWorld, to successfully pursue legislative action against Chinese producers. As members of a select few domestic producers in an industry of scale, these firms benefitted from concentrated financial gains through portraying themselves as victims of unfair trade practices. Later research expands upon Olson's hypothesis and finds that increased perceived threat, primarily in terms of declining market share, emboldens firms to "expand conflict from market to polity" (Hart, 2003). In the case of solar cells, manufacturers built a complex narrative to retain profit margins at the expense of consumers, arguing that Chinese "solar panels became job killers" while ignoring growth in the installation segment of the domestic industry (Bradsher, 2017).

Conversely, collective action dilemma renders consumers unable and disincentivized to successfully counter frame the issue, and inhibits activists opposing the message distributed by profit-driven corporations (Benford & Snow, 2000). While large scale firms have ample resources to invest in legal teams and press releases to reap the concentrated benefits of protection, American homeowners experience diffuse losses from increased pricing in solar. Although a rise in price will likely curb domestic consumption, each household bears a small segment of the financial burden and lacks the individual resources necessary to reframe the debate surrounding solar. Greater consumer mobilization and coordinated action may hypothetically succeed in representing the interests of Americans but is an unlikely solution. Tariffs typically result in significant but widespread and diffuse losses to consumers, while the few producers in the import-competing industry benefit substantially (Brock & Magee, 1978). Economic theory reinforces the roadblocks to consumer mobilization in trade policy and suggests that to effectively counter Trump's narrative, targeted messaging and engagement is necessary to mobilize an otherwise unmoved audience.

In light of the installation industry's significant growth, the manufacturing sector may face new pushback from downstream firms finding success under China's manufacturing regime. Hart (2004) asserted that individual firms pursue collective action under the duress of imminent threat. While installation has significantly expanded under affordable Chinese solar cells, the possibility of new comprehensive tariffs and a subsequent price hike certainly poses a danger to the newly successful industry. Further research on constructing counter-frames indicates that in the case of strongly held beliefs, immediate counter frames may simply reinforce the held belief, but that over time, counter-narratives may effectively erode existing frames and truly shift attitudes (Chong & Druckman, 2011). This indicates that opponents of Trump's trade policy may best structure counter-frames to engage rather than delegitimize opposing frames to prevent immediate and reactionary backlash. Framing and collective action theories could inform communication strategies adopted by the installation industry as it begins to construct a cohesive frame surrounding manufacturing, the solar industry, and domestic economic conditions. In the past, SEIA has opposed manufacturers' claims that tariffs would create and protect American jobs without significantly disrupting the industry ("Broad, Bipartisan Opposition", 2017). SEIA argues that the newly proposed tariffs will lead to a loss of over 80,000 American jobs ("Broad, Bipartisan Opposition", 2017), and has centered its messaging around the continued development of the United States solar industry as well as the expansion of residential green energy at low prices. However, their message fell short of engaging Americans across the political spectrum and failed to seriously address the grievances of unemployed blue-collar workers, instead approaching the issue from a logical, not personal, perspective. Increased fragmentation and threat perception within the domestic solar industry necessitates revisiting existing frames surrounding manufacturing and trade policy, and restructuring industry goals to reflect the needs of workers both in high tech segments of the supply chain, and manufacturing.

Firms within the solar industry are primarily responsible for creating the messaging and compiling facts to support their narrative, and the results of their analysis are then channeled through media outlets before reaching the American people. The debate surrounding the future of solar has played out throughout the past decade in news headlines, which have highlighted industrial developments and underscored the dynamic changes occurring within the industry. However, there is a great disparity in the narrative and media coverage surrounding the losses to the manufacturing sector versus the expansion of employment in highly skilled sectors, while the divide between left and right leaning news outlets isolates access to information for Americans on both sides of the aisle (Jamison, 2017). The media and political actors often engage in both framing and agenda setting, using their influence to highlight certain dimensions of an issue while overlooking others, consequently distorting public perception of the facts (Scheufele & Tewksbury, 2007). Also, research shows that resource availability is crucial to sponsor successful frames, and that consequently, frames sponsored by political and economic elites are most likely to become dominant (Gamson, Croteau, Hoynes, & Sasson, 1992). The media plays a key role in the dispersion of these frames, and evidence suggests that journalistic tendency to *define politics solely as a domain of elites* disempowers non-mainstream groups from creating a counter frame of equivalent scope and tenacity (Ryan, Carragee, & Meinhofer, 2001). These incentivized groups define what is and is not relevant to the issue (Ryan et al., 2001), and the public receives a limited base of information to draw upon when considering their political position.

In the case of solar, Trump and the manufacturing elite's frame of trade policy presents a false dichotomy of blue-collar laborers left unemployed by the evils of globalization fighting a zero sum game against multinational firms and overlooks possible alternatives for compromise and negotiation that may be against the interest of corporations but produce a better outcome for the public as a whole. Free trade, formerly accepted as a de facto positive economic policy, has become the target of policymakers seeking political support from those left behind by the inherently unequal effects of trade on low income and low skilled jobs, which would require an unlikely industrial policy strategy to ameliorate (Jacobson, 2016). This trend has been exacerbated by the current Administration throughout the past election cycle. Trump's "theory of forgotten men" weaves a narrative of small midwestern manufacturing towns ravaged by outsourcing and cheap labor, while elitist liberals in either coast profit off the gains from trade (Weingarten, 2016). Analysis of trends in media coverage in international trade further indicates that there is extensive coverage based on the interests of business elites and domestic parties interested in setting the rules for international trade, and the top-level negotiations, but limited reporting on underlying interests and motivations of the key actors involved in determining trade policy (De Sarkar & Barnes, 2006). Solar follows this pattern, with extensive coverage supporting uncompetitive domestic firms' financial interests.

These messages are dedicated to the plight of the manufacturing sector and target financially vulnerable laborers, depicted as the hardworking lifeblood of an industry unfairly plagued by relentless Chinese cost-cutting and crafty economic maneuvering. For example, the Wall Street Journal recounts the moving tale of Hickory, North Carolina, which underwent a manufacturing-driven economic renaissance, followed by a subsequent, rapid decline of industrial output and employment opportunity in the wake of the "China shock" (Hilsenrath, 2016). Poignant narratives surrounding the desolation of small-town America presume to capture the voice of unheard blue-collar communities, and appeal to those who have lost their livelihood from the apparent threat of globalization but fail to propose any long-term solution to increasing competition from already competitively superior foreign firms.

At the intersection of firm interests and the economic anxieties of the people lies the media, the conduit between the elites and the financially burdened. Throughout the recent period of increased political polarization, the "liberal media" has failed to propose an economic policy that connects with the financial anxieties of rural America (Smarsh, 2016). Past research has analyzed public perceptions of media bias; strong conservatives indeed tend to view media outlets as biased towards the left, while *the best predictor of a media bias perception is political cynicism* (Lee, 2005). Throughout the last election cycle, conservative outlets increasingly branded left-leaning publications as "fake news," pandering to blue-collar workers increasingly disillusioned by political institutions and bureaucratic processes. Liberal publications have been accused of over-intellectualization of economic turmoil and failure to create a narrative that legitimizes rural America's anxieties in a non-condescending way and proposes actionable solutions to aid the communities left behind by globalization (Tomasky, 2017).

Consequently, pro-protectionism "forgotten men" are not reached by the left's pro-trade, environmentally conscious, "elitist" narrative, and are divorced from the objective threat that tariffs on solar panels pose to their livelihoods and the environment at large. Increased accusations of media bias are primarily driven by conservative elites strategically seeking to secure their own economic interests and isolate audiences from political discourse to the detriment of cooperation and bipartisanship (Watts, Domke, Shah, & Fan, 1999). Though there is an incredible opportunity for economic development and expansion in the installation industry, its successes fail to resonate with the very individuals lacking employment. The installation industry's leaps and bounds have been covered extensively within the solar sector in an impersonal format, with media highlighting the growth in gigawatts installed and overall industrial. Recent research indicates a positive correlation between increased media coverage and adaptation of residential solar technology, but current communications strategies leave communities unexposed from competing frames and inhibit the ability of organizations and news outlets to easily spread a counter-frame opposing the narrative of conservative elites (Romeo, 2016). Engaging Americans across the aisle and facilitating actionable, pro-climate policy requires rethinking traditional media strategies and messaging tactics and tailoring the narrative to the intended audience in a way that personally connects them to the larger issues of protectionism and climate change.

Domestic producers, as the primary collectors and disseminators of information, have provided media outlets with a one-dimensional frame that furthers their financial interests without basis in unbiased research and analysis (Watts et al.,1999), while installation has yet to weave a cohesive and compelling counter-narrative due to its past lack of incentive and unfocused messaging. Furthermore, increasingly polarized media outlets inhibit the stories of one side from reaching the other, creating an ideological echo chamber incapable of catalyzing actionable change (Lee, 2005). It is crucial to present Americans with alternatives to the artificial dichotomy between manufacturing jobs and affordable imported solar panels and communicate counter-frames in a salient format that resonates with target audiences. Domestic employment and the growth of residential solar are not mutually exclusive but require a more nuanced reconciliation than simple tariffs against vertically integrated Chinese producers. The debate must be restructured from an "us vs. them" perspective, and instead address how the domestic market, with an abundance of highly skilled labor and advanced technological capabilities, can work in tandem with affordable solar to better both employment opportunities and the environment. Research suggests several tactics for bridging the gap between different views of a situation and event, and communication pathways to connect related but unsynced issues that share common goals and values. Though there are multiple processes for uniting apparently unconnected frameworks, the most effective methodologies, in the case of solar, appear to be frame bridging, amplification, and extension (Snow et al., 1986). Frame bridging involves linking congruent but unconnected ideas, and groups of people who share similar grievances but do not have the organizational capacity. Frame amplification pertains to highlighting and prioritizing values which may seem fundamental but demand redefinition and application to effect mobilization -- the goal of any social movement. Finally, frame extension entails expanding an original network to incorporate new interests and beliefs into the ultimate goal (Snow et al., 1986). Furthermore, to successfully extend and transform existing frames regarding manufacturing to engage previously disconnected constituents, it is crucial to tailor messaging towards the target audience. Past research has indicated that the success of a particular frame is largely dependent in the salience of the issue with the target audience, the ability of transmitters to provide causal analysis, draw attention to the most exigent facets of the topic, and develop potential remedies to the problem (Entman, 1993). Individuals primed to respond to an issue utilizing an ethical frame will be receptive to radically different messaging in comparison to those conditioned to analyze issues from a material, cost-benefit standpoint (Nelson & Wiley, 2001). In the case of solar, two groups emerge as primary participants in the larger narrative of the industrial divide between manufacturing and the installation industry. A key group is disillusioned blue-collar workers themselves, suspicious and fearful of Chinese competition, and consequently receptive to Trump's anti-trade and anti-climate narrative (Bradsher, 2017). These individuals have been engaged with an ethical frame that emphasizes traditional value systems, and counter-framing strategy should legitimize their economic anxiety while aligning with existing morals and beliefs. Conversely, communication strategies that emphasize material frames will be most effective in engaging individuals already supportive of solar expansion but unaware of the ramifications of trade policy in affordable residential solar, and the environment as a whole.

Trump's dogmatic emphasis on manufacturing as a cornerstone of the American economy enables the narrative of manufacturing firms while providing blue-collar workers with obfuscating information regarding their very livelihoods. Throughout his campaign, Trump drew strong support from an ever-growing voter base through false promises of job recovery and the revitalization of Factory America – both in terms of economic security and social dignity (Bein-Khan, 2016). These workers, predominantly white men without college degrees, have faced increasing economic uncertainty due to declining job opportunities beginning in the 1980s. Surveys indicate "the share of men between 25 and 54 who are neither working nor looking for work [also known as the inactivity rate] has increased with each passing decade" (Thompson, 2016b, par 18) Jobs have shifted to service focused industries, while wages for individuals without college degrees have fallen 13 percent since the 1990s (Thompson, 2016b). This increasingly impoverished voting base was moved by Trump's emotional and ethical appeal for conservative trade policy and feigned support for the conservative, traditional values that characterize the rural manufacturing towns across the Midwest. These workers were primed to ethically evaluate determinations based on rights, morals, and basic principles, and are consequently less likely to adopt a compensatory stance that is receptive to compromise (Abramson & Inglehart, 1995). Consequently, messaging must address their biases regarding the benefits of trade and the impact of tariffs in not only the American economy, the solar industry, but especially their everyday lives.

While these individuals may not be motivated by a desire to combat climate change or maintain industrial growth in the installation sector, it is still possible to engage them and counter their assumptions regarding the economic and environmental costs of tariffs by amplifying existing frames to expand upon the relationship between manufacturing jobs and the solar industry (Snow et al., 1986). Tariffs are fundamentally a tax on imported goods and are a form of government meddling in a market economy. Conservative elites are able to take advantage of these workers' political cynicism and further polarize trade policy debate, (Watts et al., 1999) but effective counter-frames could use the same economic anxiety as a call to bipartisan action due to the exigent nature of the situation. Potential messaging could stress the uncertainty of intervening in a growing industry, and the potential for overall collapse should demand for panels significantly drop in light of a price hike.

While pro-trade segments of the solar industry have typically stressed industry successes in the past, transformation of the pro-trade frame to address and relate to anxieties of those hurt by globalization will destabilize the manufacturing industry's monopoly over blue-collar worker's votes, and include these individuals in the larger narrative of progressive solar policy rather than marginalizing their experiences (Snow et al., 1986). Further tariffs and protection in line with the Trump agenda certainly threaten to destabilize solar panel imports from China. The entire industry will be shaken, and the very manufacturing jobs that domestic producers are attempting to "protect" with impending litigation may disappear regardless. These taxes on panels could easily destroy the future of American solar due to their comprehensive nature, and in a worst-case scenario, leave unskilled workers unemployed and destitute (Hill, 2017). Families seeking job security from heightened protection will be receptive to the message that further protectionist policy - in the form of government-imposed taxes nonetheless- will only create further instability and uncertainty, and ultimately result in widespread job loss -and possible collapse - for the industry as a whole.

However, the narrative must be conveyed by an appropriate messenger able to resonate with American manufacturing without appearing erudite or disconnected from the working class. Many of these individuals feel that they do not have a voice in the political sphere, and it is unlikely that they will be receptive to the narrative of a perceived outsider (Thompson, 2016a). Consequently, to engage blue collar workers mired in an ethical anti-trade frame, the current pro-solar frame must transform to incorporate key values of the rural working class to increase the relatability and saliency of the pro-solar position (Snow et al., 1986). Messengers with whom the target audience is already familiar are more accessible to an audience and have more success in activating and applying existing ideas to the new frame (Scheufele & Tewksbury, 2007). Through careful selection of a messenger who bridges the gap between policy and personal experience, it is possible to connect the needs of these unemployed workers with the objectives of pro-solar organizations.

In light of the contentious Solar 201 litigation, conservative Senators have spoken out against further trade barriers, particularly Senator Tom Tillis of North Carolina, arguing that the "protection" stipulated by tariffs will significantly hurt the state economy despite the allegations of domestic manufacturers (Murawski, 2017). Tillis has already spoken out against further protection, arguing that "The tariffs would especially hurt residential rooftop solar projects that are growing rapidly. Increasing costs will stop solar growth dead in its tracks, threatening tens of thousands of American workers in the solar industry" (Murawski, 2017). Established Republican politicians like Tillis have the potential to assuage the anxieties of blue-collar workers by affirming that trade barriers will only serve to destabilize the industry and put thousands of jobs in grave peril. Messaging that legitimizes the fears of manufacturing workers, provides viable solutions, and is delivered by an appropriate spokesperson may successfully reach the very demographic most supportive of Trump's protectionist policies.

On the other hand, affluent, eco-conscious consumers who purchase the final solar product for residential use are more concerned with their environmental impact and price of the end product than job security. These voters make decisions using a material-based framework and likely have adopted a compensatory position that allows for tradeoffs between positive and negative aspects of the issue (Abramson & Ingelhart, 1995). Consequently, messaging that highlights the benefits of pro-solar policy from an empirical, quantitative perspective will be most effective in engaging and motivating these individuals to vote and advocate for a continuation of accessible residential solar (Nelson & Wiley, 2001). Existing research highlights key tactics to engage this demographic in the solar market and suggests successful methods of cultivating a committed and engaged consumer base. Emphasizing the affordability and reliability of residential solar via cohesive industry-wide message results in consumer retention and aids in overcoming the market barriers that inhibit expansion of green energy (Ambepitiya, 2015). Research conducted by SolarCity, a green energy provider, indicates that consumers are interested in supporting environmentally conscious, socially responsible, and sustainability-focused businesses (SolarCity, 2014). Messaging highlighting the positive environmental and ethical contributions of firms in the solar industry will promote engagement and investment in green technology and taps into the consumer bases' desire to appear socially and ethically conscious (SolarCity, 2014).

However, social pressure and environmental consciousness come with a price attached, and while green-minded societal norms may contribute to increased demand, economic cost ultimately determines who is willing and able to pay for residential solar technology. While blue-collar workers may not feel the direct impact of Chinese tariffs on their purchasing power, green-minded consumers looking to enter the residential solar community are directly affected by price fluctuations -- as the price of panels fell, their demand grew, and were the price of solar to rise, it will fall (Honeyman, 2017). Consequently, it is crucial to educate potential consumers in the environmental benefits of green technology adaptation while underscoring the effects of tariffs on price, thus playing into existing material frames and tailoring counter-frames to their existing method of judgement (Nelson & Wiley, 2001). This demographic of consumers may be more receptive to the message of organizations like SEIA, which are concerned with both industry growth and environmental protection. SEIA's research regarding tariffs, demand, and the environment paints a poignant image of a future without affordable solar, and the resulting environmental degradation. The ominous forecast for the future of solar energy and climate change may successfully mobilize consumers to advocate against Trump's trade policy and take action in the policy sphere, be it organizing local coalitions in support of green energy, rallying for affordable solar, or submitting constituent letters. Messaging should center around educating aspirational consumers on the future of solar technology and expansion through underscoring the substantial environmental benefits of solar technology versus the potential spike in carbon emissions, and the subsequent impact on climate change should the solar industry contract during the aftermath of increased tariffs.

Ultimately, China's unprecedented increase in manufacturing capability provides the United States solar industry the ability to restructure and reorient itself towards the future; a domestic energy industry driven by highly skilled labor and solar installation. Without a significant decrease in the price of CSPV cells, residential solar would not have grown in affordability, and the installation industry as Americans know it would be significantly less successful. Domestic firms would do well to take advantage of the advent of residential solar and build off of China's research and development in highly skilled segments of the solar supply chain. The misguided narrative that America must return to its past manufacturing roots only stymies economic growth in profitable sectors of the industry, inhibits the creation of future jobs, and ignores the real threat of climate change.

Engaging both blue-collar workers and environmentally oriented consumers with the implementation of solar technology and forward-thinking energy policy requires a ground-up approach that begins with reorienting messaging strategies to focus on the needs of specific groups of people. While Trump's campaign promoted political polarization and divided the American population, solar technology has the capability to unite constituents across the aisle. The divided media's portrayal of low skilled blue-collar workers engaged in a zero-sum economic struggle against coastal liberal elites creates a false dichotomy between two groups of people who ultimately have the same common interest; economic prosperity and a greener future. Though domestic manufacturers have had years to construct a story that caters to the insecurities of the very individuals they employ, while the installation industry has yet to create a strong cohesive narrative, there is hope for a united message stemming from an unlikely partnership between pro-market Republicans and other segments of the solar industry, who share a mutual goal of preserving jobs and promoting sensible long term energy policy to the benefit of both the environment and the economy. Despite the impending danger that the 201 Safeguard tariff poses to the industry, the perceived threat of heightened protection may incentivize bipartisanship in an increasingly divided industry and necessitate progressive partnership to counter the narrative of an inefficient industry and divisive Administration.

References

Abramson, P. & Inglehart, R. (1995). *Value change in global perspective: A Comprehensive examination of global attitude changes.* Ann Arbor, Michigan. University of Michigan Press.

Ambepitiya, K. (2015). Strategies to promote solar power energy: A Review of literature. *Proceedings of 8th International Research Conference,* 249-255.

Atkinson, R. D., Steward, L.A., Andes, S. M., & Ezell S.J. (2012). Worse than the great depression: What experts are missing about American manufacturing decline. *The Information Technology & Innovation Foundation.* Retrieved from http://www2.itif.org/2012-american-manufacturing-decline.pdf

Ball, J., Reicher, D., Sun, X., Pollock, C. (2017). The new Solar System. *Steyer-Taylor Center for Energy Policy and Finance,* 1-213.

Bein-Khan, J. (2016, December 7). Trump can't deliver the Rust Belt jobs he promised because work has changed. *Wired.* Retrieved from https://www.wired.com/2016/12/trump-cant-deliver-rust-belt-jobs-work-changed/

Benford, R., & Snow, D. (2000). Framing processes and social movements: An overview and assessment. *Annual Review of Sociology, 26,* 611-639. https://doi.org/10.1146/annurev.soc.26.1.611

Bradsher, K. (April 8, 2017). When solar panels became job killers. *New York Times.* Retrieved from https://www.nytimes.com/2017/04/08/business/china-trade-solar-panels.html

Brock, W., & Magee, S. (1978). The economics of special interest politics: The case of the tariff. *The American Economic Review, 68*(2), 246-250.

Broad, Bipartisan Opposition to Solar Tariffs as ITC Hears Trade Case. (2017, August 15). Retrieved from https://www.seia.org/news/broad-bipartisan-opposition-solar-tariffs-itc-hears-trade-case

Chong, D., & Druckman, J. (2007). Framing theory. *Annual Review Political Science,* 103-126. https://doi.org/10.1146/annurev.polisci.10.072805.103054

Dana, R. (2017, June 19). Where does Trump stand on solar? *Solar Tribune.* Retrieved from https://solartribune.com/where-does-trump-stand-on-solar/

De Sarkar, D., & Barnes, J. (2006). Trade challenges, media challenges: strengthening trade coverage beyond the headlines. *World Trade Organization Public Forum,* 1-12.

Entman, R. (1993). Framing: Toward clarification of a fractured paradigm. *Journal of Communication, 43*(4), 51-57. https://doi.org/10.1111/j.1460-2466.1993.tb01304.x

Gamson, W., Croteau, D., Hoynes, D., & Sasson, T. (1992). Media images and the social construction of reality. *Annual Review of Sociology, 95,* 1-37. http://dx.doi.org/10.1146/annurev.so.18.080192.002105

Greenhouse, S. (2016). Donald Trump's appeal to Rust Belt workers. *New York Times.* Retrieved from https://www.nytimes.com/2016/07/03/opinion/sunday/donald-trumps-appeal-to-rust-belt-workers.html

Goodrich, A. C., Powell, D. M., James, T. L., Woodhouse, M., Buonassisi, T. (2013). Assessing the drivers of regional trends in solar photovoltaic manufacturing. *The Royal Society of Chemistry, 6,* 2811-2821.

Hart, D. M. (2004). Political representation in concentrated industries: Revisiting the "Olsonian Hypothesis". *Business and Politics, 5,* 1077-1077. https://doi.org/10.2202/1469-3569.1077

Hill, J. (2017, August 29). Trump demand for tariffs bad news for US solar industry. *Clean Technica.* Retrieved from https://cleantechnica.com/2017/08/29/trump-demand-tariffs-bad-news-us-solar-industry/

Hilsenrath, B. D. (2016, August 11). How the China shock, deep and swift, spurred the rise of Trump. *The Wall Street Journal.* Retrieved from https://www.wsj.com/articles/how-the-china-shock-deep-and-swift-spurred-the-rise-of-trump-1470929543

Honeyman, C. (2017, June). U.S. solar outlook under Section 201: The trade case's impact on U.S. solar demand. *GreenTech Media.* Retrieved from https://www.greentechmedia.com/research/report/us-solar-outlook-under-section-201

Inslee, J. (2017, September 10). No place for climate change deniers to hide. *Huffington Post.* Retrieved from https://www.huffingtonpost.com/entry/no-place-for-climate-change-deniers-to-hide_us_59b55cc4e4b0b5e53106ca87

Jacobson, L. (2017, September 12). How free trade became a political liability. *Governing Magazine.* Retrieved from http://www.governing.com/topics/elections/gov-free-trade-trump-clinton-sanders.html

Jamison, M. (April 12, 2017). The great media divide: News business models on the right and left perpetuate our political divide. *The American Enterprise Institute.* Retrieved from http://www.aei.org/publication/the-great-media-divide/

Kennedy, B. (2016, October 05). Americans strongly favor expanding solar power to help address costs and environmental concerns. *Pew Research Center.* Retrieved from http://www.pewresearch.org/fact-tank/2016/10/05/americans-strongly-favor-expanding-solar-power-to-help-address-costs-and-environmental-concerns/

Lee, T. (2005). The liberal media myth revisited: An examination of factors influencing perceptions of media bias. *Journal of Broadcasting & Electronic Media, 49(1)*, 43-64. https://doi.org/10.1207/s15506878jobem4901_4

Levin, B. (2017, August 28). Trump's tariff tantrum makes Veruca Salt look like the Dalai Lama. *Vanity Fair.* Retrieved from https://article.wn.com/view/2017/08/29/Trump_s_Tariff_Tantrum_Makes_Veruca_Salt_Look_Like_the_Dalai/

Marshall, C., Storrow, B., Reilly, S., & Northey, H. (2017, May 5). Solar: Tariffs would hurt demand 'significantly' - Goldman Sachs. *GreenWire.* Retrieved from https://www.eenews.net/greenwire

Matsuyama, K. (2009). Structural change in an interdependent world: A global view of manufacturing decline. *Journal of the European Economic Association, 7(2-3)*, 478–486. https://doi.org/10.1162/JEEA.2009.7.2-3.478

Meyer R. (2017, August 28). Trump and the Paris Agreement: What just happened? *The Atlantic.* Retrieved from https://www.theatlantic.com/science/archive/2017/08/trump-and-the-paris-agreement-what-just-happened/536040/

Miles, T. (2017, May 29). U.S. may put emergency tariffs on solar imports. *Reuters.* Retrieved from https://www.reuters.com/article/us-usa-solar-wto-idUSKBN18P1JL

Murawski, J. (2017, August 16). NC Republicans rally to save state's solar industry. *News Observer.* Retrieved from http://www.newsobserver.com/news/business/article167582022.html

Nelson, T., & Wiley, E. (2001). Issue frames that strike a value balance: A political psychology perspective (pp. 245-267). In Stephen D. Reese, Oscar H. Gandy, Jr., & August E. Grant (Eds.) *Framing Public Life, Perspectives in Media and Our Understanding of the Social World.* Mahwah, NJ: Laurence Earlbaum

Osborne, M. (2013, January 14). ENF: Over 300 small Chinese solar companies stopped operating in 2012. *PV-Tech.* Retrieved from https://www.pv-tech.org/news/over_300_small_chinese_solar_companies_stopped_operating_in_2012_says_enf

Page, S. (2017, May 20). Amid layoffs and bankruptcies, solar renegades turn to Trump to fight 'China'. *ThinkProgress.* Retrieved from https://thinkprogress.org/suniva-trade-case-48252a50c0dc/

Powell, D., Fu, R., Horowitz, K., Basore, P. Woodhouse, S., Buonassisi, T. (2015). The capital intensity of photovoltaics manufacturing: barrier to scale and opportunity for innovation. *Royal Society of Chemistry, Energy and Environmental Science,* 8, 3395-3408. DOI: 10.1039/C5EE01509J

Reuter, G. & Kuebler, M. (2017, June 17). China leading the way in solar energy expansion as renewables surge. *Deutsche Welle.* Retrieved from http://www.dw.com/en/china-leading-the-way-in-solar-energy-expansion-as-renewables-surge/a-39081117

Romeo, C. (2016). Media effects on solar panel installations across 20 states. *Journal of Environmental and Resource Economics at Colby, 3*(1).

Rosenfeld, E. (2017, August 28). Trump reportedly demands China action: 'I want tariffs. And I want someone to bring me some tariffs'. *CNBC.* Retrieved from https://www.cnbc.com/2017/08/27/trump-reportedly-demands-china-action-i-want-tariffs-and-i-want-someone-to-bring-me-some-tariffs.html

Ryan, C., Carragee, K. M., & Meinhofer, W. (2001). Theory into practice: Framing, the news media, and collective action. *Journal of Broadcasting & Electronic Media, 45*(1), 175-182. https://doi.org/10.1207/s15506878jobem4501_11

Ryan, J. (2017, June 26). Tariffs on solar panels could slow industry growth by 66%. *Bloomberg News*. Retrieved from https://www.bloomberg.com/news/articles/2017-06-26/tariffs-on-solar-panels-seen-slowing-industry-growth-by-6

Ryan, J. & Dlouhy, J. A. (2017, June 15). This case could upend America's $29 billion solar industry. *Bloomberg News*. Retrieved from https://www.bloomberg.com/news/articles/2017-06-15/this-case-could-upend-america-s-29-billion-solar-industry

Scheufele, D. & Tewksbury, D. (2007). Framing, agenda setting, and priming. The evolution of three media effects models. *Journal of Communication, 57*, 9-20. https://doi.org/10.1111/j.0021-9916.2007.00326.x

Smarsh, S. (2016, October 13). Dangerous idiots: how the liberal media elite failed working-class Americans. *The Guardian*. Retrieved from https://www.theguardian.com/media/2016/oct/13/liberal-media-bias-working-class-americans

Snow, D., Burke, R., Wordon, S., & Benford, R. (1986). Frame alignment processes, micromobilization, and movement. *American Sociological Review, 51*(4), 464-481. DOI: 10.2307/2095581

SolarCity. (2014). Consumer trends in sustainability: Insights to grow your market share and defend your brand. Retrieved from http://www.solarcity.com/newsroom/reports/consumer-trends-sustainability

Solar Energy Industry Association (2014, December 26). *The solar industry: Upstream vs. downstream*. Retrieved from https://seekingalpha.com/article/2781835-the-solar-industry-upstream-vs-downstream

Solar Panel Installation (2017). *The Solar Company*. Retrieved from https://www.thesolarco.com/

Solar Section 201 Case - Frequently Asked Questions (n.d.). Retrieved from https://www.seia.org/initiatives/solar-section-201-case-frequently-asked-questions

Sufrin, S. C. & Olson, M. (1966). The logic of collective action: Public goods and the theory of groups. *Industrial and Labor Relations Review, 19*(4), 640.

The Solar Foundation (2016). National Solar Jobs Census 2016. Retrieved from https://www.thesolarfoundation.org/national/

Thompson, D. (2016a, March 01). Who are Donald Trump's supporters, really? *The Atlantic*. Retrieved from https://www.theatlantic.com/politics/archive/2016/03/who-are-donald-trumps-supporters-really/471714/

Thompson, D. (2016b, May 13). Donald Trump and the twilight of White America. *The Atlantic*. Retrieved from https://www.theatlantic.com/politics/archive/2016/05/donald-trump-and-the-twilight-of-white-america/482655/

Tomasky, M. (2017, May 30). Elitism Is liberalism's biggest problem. *New Republic*. Retrieved from https://newrepublic.com/article/142372/elitism-liberalisms-biggest-problem

Varian, H. (2001). High-technology industries and market structure. Proceedings of the Economic Policy Symposium - Jackson Hole 2018 (pp. 65-101). Kansas City: Federal Reserve Bank.

Watts, M. D., Domke, D., Shah, D. V., & Fan, D. P. (1999). Elite cues and media bias in presidential campaigns. *Communication Research, 26*(2), 144-175. https://doi.org/10.1177/009365099026002003

Weingarten, B. (2016, August 26). Creative destruction and the decline of low skilled labor in America. *Encounter Books*. Retrieved from https://www.encounterbooks.com/features/upside-creative-destruction-wrought-trade-small-town-america/

Zhao, Q. (2015). *Services in global value chains: Solar panel manufacturing in China*. Retrieved from http://www.intracen.org/uploadedFiles/intracenorg/Content/Publications/solarpanel%20-full-web%20(2).pdf

Chapter 7

Key Strategic Climate Denial Techniques Journalists Should Understand

Jasper Fessmann, PhD

Introduction

Strategic public relations (PR) professionals working on behalf of vested oil and gas interests have been successful at shaping public opinion on climate change for thirty years. Through their work, they have been able to sustain the status quo and stop possible action to mitigate the threat of anthropogenic climate change. As discussed in chapter 1, many climate change communications campaigns in the past have attempted to address the issue from an information-deficit model approach of trying to raise awareness in the hope that providing scientific facts will change opinions and encourage action. This has not worked as expected and runs counter to studies in behavioral psychology (i.e. Foxall, 1990).

Journalists often operate in information-deficit models of climate change reporting. They are also vulnerable to manipulation by fossil-fuel PR professionals exhibiting a war mindset (Fessmann, 2018) according to which achieving their ends justified by any means. As professional climate denier Marc Morano put it: *"You can't be afraid of the absolute hand-to-hand combat, metaphorically"* (Kenner & Robledo, 2014, min 1:04). Such hardball strategies have been highly effective in getting journalists to adopt false and misleading reporting, too often without the journalists realizing the manipulation.

In this chapter, I look at the problems of climate journalism from an outsider perspective of a public interest communications (PIC) (Fessmann, 2016; 2017) scholar. Based on my twenty years of experience as a PR practitioner, including running my own PR agency for twelve years, this chapter shows some of the most effective media manipulation techniques employed by professional climate denial strategists and offers some suggestions on how to counter them. The overall goal is to offer my perspective as a PR professional to journalists looking to raise their resistance to those techniques. As a PR professional, I argue that journalists need to recognize that the misleading presentation by climate change denier "experts" is a well-planned, deliberate strategic communications strategy, taking advantage of professional challenges such as vastly underfunded newsrooms, and uncritical adherence to the objectivity-principle in journalism.

Professional climate change deniers understand the journalists they are dealing with, but journalists often don't understand the games the deniers play. PR practitioners are routinely trained to understand journalists, write like them and anticipate their thinking—the core media relations strategy in PR. Conceptually, PR fulfills what is called the *information subsidy role* (Gandy, 1982)—saving journalists time and effort by providing ready-made texts and stories to journalists in return for name recognition of the PR client or company. The food analogy would be TV dinners or fast food, not the healthiest option but gets the job done if in a rush (which journalists perpetually are in, and that's getting worse).

This understanding of journalism by PR professionals is not reciprocated by journalists, who are rarely trained in strategic communications – which is by most journalists seen as too near to advocacy and thus not compatible with journalistic ethos. As a result, there is a strong imbalance in the relative understanding and analysis of the situation. As the ancient Chinese general Sun Tzu (1910) put it:

> *If you know the enemy and know yourself, you need not fear the result of a hundred battles. If you know yourself but not the enemy, for every victory gained you will also suffer a defeat. If you know neither the enemy nor yourself, you will succumb in every battle.* (Tzu, 1910, p. 11)

Often journalists only know themselves (and their trade). Thus, strategic communicators who understand both the opposition (fossil fuel PR companies) and themselves will be more successful at communicating this issue. Such a systematic, strategic approach lies at the heart of climate change denial in the United States, which succeeded in stopping meaningful action on climate change for at least thirty years.

Journalists, therefore, should understand the strategies employed by strategic communicators and learn to anticipate them to counter this PR advantage and balance the scales even though the journalistic value of *objectivity* may prevent journalists from using the techniques themselves. To use a card-playing analogy, it is useful to know how people cheat in card games to spot such attempts even though one does not intend to employ the trick themselves.

Using the "activist" label and "journalistic objectivity" to manipulate journalists

PR professionals know that journalists reject being called activists. Most journalists feel that being an activist fundamentally conflicts with core journalistic principles, especially objectivity. These feelings by journalists are a core weakness that strategic communicators for climate denial ruthlessly exploit. These communicators know that labeling a journalist an "activist" leads journalists to engage in behaviors to avoid the charge of lacking objectivity—pushing the journalist in the direction wanted by the professional communicator. Thus, in order to present a "balanced" view of the issue, climate deniers are given equal space in media coverage as scientists representing the consensus reached by 98% of peer-reviewed research (see chapter 2). So, paradoxically in an attempt to preserve (the appearance of) journalistic objectivity, the objective truth on climate change is constantly undermined.

Journalism schools and programs in the United States typically train their students to see objectivity (or at least efforts towards it) as a central concept in their work. At the same time, it is recognized that pure objectivity can never fully be achieved because human beings and news organizations have built-in implicit biases and see the events in the world through specific mental frames. Thus, serious journalists work hard on being as objective as possible in their reporting. As the preamble of the Society of Professional Journalists code of ethics states that members believe that:

> *Public enlightenment is the forerunner of justice and the foundation of democracy. The duty of the journalist is to further those ends by seeking truth and providing a fair and comprehensive account of events and issues. Conscientious journalists ... strive to serve the public with thoroughness and honesty.* ("Code of Ethics", 1996, par 1)

The goal of trying to be objective is thus central to the journalistic ethos and when applied with due diligence, thoroughness and honesty a great strength of journalism and pillar of democracy. However, in an age of alternative facts, the way media is used to display "both sides" factually hurts the truth and the credibility of the media itself. False claims are routinely given the mantle of truth by allowing them equal time and standing, even when a scientific consensus is evident. The tenet of objectivity has been used by strategic climate change deniers to great effect in manipulating journalists. The most common example of this on television is the split screen or dialogue between a climate scientist and so-called climate change sceptic. As John Oliver put it in his illuminating report on climate change:

*I think I know why people think this issue [anthropogenic climate change] is still open to debate. Because **on TV it is**. And it is always one person for, one person against. ... at the screen it is 50:50 [%] which is inherently misleading.* (Last Week Tonight with John Oliver, 2014, May 11, 2:11-2:22, emphasis in the original)

PR's effectiveness in deliberately creating such false-balance presentations is grounded in techniques developed by PR agencies such as Hill+Knowlton Strategies for the tobacco industry and later other industries (Kenner & Robledo, 2014): to deny cancer research, to deny the effects of pesticides for the chemical industry and finally deny human-caused climate change for the oil/gas industry. The application of these techniques was a significant factor in creating the current fake news phenomenon and the dramatic decline in trust in the mainstream media. However, that is at the core not just the fault of PR. Journalism bears equal responsibility for the situation by not adapting to and learning from the other side. This includes learning not to be bullied by the "activist" or "not objective" labels.

A promising response to this challenge that emerged in the early 2000s is "solutions journalism." Solutions journalism focuses its news reporting not only on the issue but also on the responses that have been taken or could be taken to address the issues. Solutions stories are grounded in credible scientific and empirical evidence and explore how and why approaches to fix the problem discussed work or don't work. As the Solutions Journalism Network (2018) describes it:

Audiences regularly come away from the news — even high-quality news — feeling powerless, anxious, and resentful. Solutions journalism heightens accountability by reporting on where and how people are doing better against a problem... It offers ... society self-correct, spotlighting adaptive responses that people and communities can learn from. (pars. 1-3)

Solutions journalism may also offer an answer to one of the biggest problems overall in climate change communications—its inherent negativity. The threat of catastrophic climate change by its nature is very, very scary. Climate change reporting often describes the potentially apocalyptical results of global warming and climate change without providing solutions, leaving the readers/viewers/listeners alone with the fears created. This naturally creates *cognitive dissonance* (Festinger,1957) and individuals need to find a way to deal with it, often by denial. Offering solutions instead focuses the audience's mental energy on the solutions that provide hope.

One key example of promising climate-solutions journalism is *Project Drawdown* (Hawken, 2017). Project Drawdown (and its corresponding, same-titled book) lists and ranks solution-by-solution one hundred already existing approaches to climate change and scales them up to their logical potential. It finds that many of the solutions proposed, calculated over the next twenty or so years, are actually more economical than continued use of existing technologies, especially fossil fuel-based technologies. This counters a core denial argument that it would simply be too expensive and too uneconomical to do something about climate change. Given the scope of *Drawdown* and other such projects, there are enough solutions that a journalist could always find a solution to dedicate a paragraph to in any major climate change story, making the story much more meaningful and responsible. Cumulatively, hundreds of such stories could have a major impact in making people aware that solutions do exist, providing hope and give the population a sense of self-efficacy (the feeling that they can take action to address a problem) (Bandura, 1977; 1982)—in turn fueling activism.

However, as promising as the "solutions journalism" approach is, it needs to be noted that each solution offered will be opposed by vested interest whose business model relies on the status quo. This means, strategic communicators on the business's behalf will fight the solutions—and that solution journalists will only be effective if they understand strategic communications.

Proposed solutions:

1. Journalists should read up on PR techniques and develop a strategic outlook.

2. Journalists should become more conscious of how the "activist" label is used against them to undermine the objective truth—and accept that it is no truer than the journalist being "enemies of the people."

3. Journalists should not give climate deniers a forum for their unsubstantiated views.

4. Journalism classes should incorporate strategic communications aspects into the curriculum and invite PR professors for guest lectures.

5. Journalism schools should require journalism students to take at least one public relations/strategic communications course to better understand the strategic outlook of public relations,

learning when PR is a legitimate ally that can provide great benefits for a journalist and when PR is used actively against journalism.

6.   More journalists should embrace the "solutions journalism" approach.

7.   As a new journalistic principle, each negative climate change story should be balanced with a discussion of at least one positive solution.

8.   If possible, stories should also include one crystal-clear call-to-action on one aspect to elevate the situation.

"Kooks:" Dealing with ego-driven climate change deniers

Part of the problem for climate science and journalistic reporting is that some genuine scientists such as Fred Singer made up their mind about the question of climate change as an anthropogenic phenomenon at a time when indeed the science was not yet clear. Instead of re-examining the evidence logically and objectively (scientifically), such individuals defend the once-adopted position with ever more spurious data in order to avoid having to admit that they were wrong. The original scientific uncertainty and genuine (but irrational) belief in climate change denial made such (former) scientists like Singer seem credible for many audiences. The media routinely accepts them as authorities, trusting in their scientific conclusions. These (usually former) scientists are effectively used by strategic climate deniers to lend their pseudo-scientific denial arguments the appearance of real science. For the former scientist themselves, usually pensioners now, such engagements are attractive since they offer attention, flattery and income where there is none left in academia (since they are not producing scientific work anymore).

Similarly, journalists are often offered other scientists as "experts" by deniers just because they have an academic degree—typically from academic disciplines other than climate science which do not necessarily qualify them to comment on climatology. Given the highly-specialized academic scholarship of climate science, a physics or engineering professor is usually not much more qualified to comment on climate change than a layperson. This is like asking a car mechanic to repair and maintain the engines of a 747 Airliner—resulting most likely in a crash. While a basic understanding of science and common sense should make the lack of qualification clear to the journalists, in the news media such scientists are often given almost equal credibility as "experts" as true climate scientists.

Members of both these groups—former scientists who have since fallen out of touch with the current literature on the climate topic, and scientists without the training to credibly comment on climate issues—I label *ego driven climate change deniers* because their sense of importance and discounting of the possibility that they may be wrong drives much of their denial. In a strict sense, they have abandoned the scientific method which requires dispassionate weighing of the evidence. Thus, they are no longer true scientists but former practitioners or unqualified to comment at all on the issues.

By any objective measure, the *ego-driven climate change deniers'* claims are not accurate, and no newspaper or media outlet claiming to adhere to the journalistic creed or code of ethics should give them a forum to present their views. This is not because these individuals shouldn't have the right to express their opinions—they certainly do— but rather because journalism claims to value accuracy and facts and it is unethical to present the public with sources that claim to be credible but are not. For example, members of the Flat Earth Society (https://theflatearthsociety.org/home/) claim that the earth is actually flat (arguing that the moon landings and transcontinental flights are elaborate hoaxes). These are justifiably not given the same credibility as members of the esteemed Royal Society of London for Improving Natural Knowledge (commonly known as the Royal Society), the world's oldest independent scientific academy. There is no reason grounded in facts why climate change deniers should be given more voice than flat-earthers in the media. Journalist and news outlets that do it anyway should be called out for it by organizations working towards journalistic values and treated with contempt—bringing journalistic peer-pressure to bear.

This is also true for the opinion pages of newspapers. Editorials in major news outlets carry the credibility of the newspaper because their inclusion is based on the assumption of the article coming from subject matter experts whose conclusions are based on facts, whether or not the news outlet agrees with the conclusions reached. In this light, the decision of the *Wall Street Journal* on May 15, 2018 to give its editorial page to 93-year-old science contrarian and climate denier Fred Singer damages the credibility of WSJ. In the opinion piece, Singer argued that *"The Sea Is Rising, but Not Because of Climate Change - There is nothing we can do about it, except to build dikes and sea walls a little bit higher"* (Singer, 2018, par 1). The response by climate scientists is best captured by a Twitter post from Michael Mann, Professor and Director of the Earth System Science Center at Penn State: *"Stay tuned for these great followup @WSJ op-eds: "Objects are falling, but Not Because of Gravity" "Continents are moving, but Not Because of Plate Tectonics"* (MichaelEMann, 2018).

The "science" that Singer's article claimed to be based on was—and had long been—debunked, but the article still may have caused damage to science similar to the scientific study that linked autism with vaccination, sparking the anti-vaccination movement that has become a dangerous health threat. Though debunked, both are and will be regularly quoted and used to persuade those who don't know better. The *Wall Street Journal* bears the responsibility for this. Such editorial influence based on vested interest will continue unless it starts to affect the profits of the WSJ through a lost reputation for good journalism and objectivity.

Proposed solutions:

1. Journalists should reject ego-driven climate change deniers as sources and make this part of professional practice.

2. The media should accept the "kook-status" of climate deniers and treat them accordingly—do not accord them any credibility.

3. Scientists should make clear that these ego-driven climate change deniers don't use the scientific methods and thus don't deserve to be called scientists on this issue—just opinion peddlers better suited to blog posts.

4. Both groups should not shy away from making these points clear even though they will feel uncomfortable calling into question another's journalistic or scientific credibility.

There is no truth – Exploiting an inherent communications weakness in science

A fundamental problem in communicating scientific facts is that the scientific method inherently never gives ultimate answers. Any scientific fact is provisional in the sense that it is a judgement based on the best available evidence at the time. It can never provide capital "T" Truth. For example, for a long time, Newtonian physics were seen as the best possible science – for most people seen as the Truth. Then, Albert Einstein's theory of relativity showed that Newton was wrong. The scientific method is a road on which we will never be able to ultimately arrive at the destination of Truth, just approaching it. This was clear even to philosophers such Francis Bacon and other Enlightenment thinkers who first formulated the scientific method to gain knowledge: scientific facts are hypotheses that have stood the test of time and have not yet been disproven – small "t" truths. There is no Truth in science, only increased confidence that the theories may be right. The problem here is that this aspect of science receives little attention. Furthermore, such understanding runs counter to the human psychological need for clarity and closure – we are hardwired to avoid uncertainty.

Because of the inherent limitations of scientific methods regarding providing certainty, scientists are trained and conditioned not to express data in absolute terms. This uncertainty is one of the most potent weapons yielded in climate change denial: you often hear such things as *the science is just not in yet*. For example, 28% of the US population believes "that there is a lot of disagreement" among climate scientists on the issue and 26% have "somewhat/strong mistrust" of climate scientists (Howe, Mildenberger, Marlon, & Leiserowitz, 2015).

So, were these doubts justified? While there may still have been legitimate doubts about man-made climate change deeply affecting our climate and weather in the 1980-90s, by now man-made climate change is one of the most repetitively proven scientific facts. 97-100% (depending on the specific meta-analysis) of climate scientists agree that man-made climate change is real. Furthermore, all recent climate change models that have been developed and computer tested, require to take man-made climate influences into account in order to be consistent with the actually observed weather patterns since the 1950s. Man-made climate change is thus the dominant paradigm (Kuhn, 2012) of climate science and a scientific fact. The point here is that while there still is a miniscule group of doubters in the scientific community the "**science is in**". Climate change deniers deserve no more media credit and attention than those who argue against Darwin's theory of evolution, believe Einstein was wrong or are members of the Flat Earth Society. Any scientific field produces a small number of habitual contrarians and *kooks* – only in climate science are they taken seriously by much of the media.

The issue of not being able to provide absolute truth is not limited to science – it is also a core issue in criminal justice. There, like in science, the objective Truth is desired but unobtainable – even in cases with criminals confessing, their testimony sometimes turned out to be false. To deal with the issue, the legal profession has developed two standards of proof:

a)   the preponderance of evidence in civil matters

b)   evidence of guilt beyond a reasonable doubt in criminal cases

These are useful standards to employ on the scientific status of man-made climate change as well: In the 1980s there was a preponderance of evidence pointing to man-made climate change. Since the 2000s we have enough evidence that it is beyond any reasonable doubt.

From a framing standpoint (Goffman, 1974; Snow & Benford, 1998; Benford & Snow, 2000) the global warming controversy is "a framing contest between the environmental establishment, and, among others, the conservative movement" (McCright & Dunlap, 2000, p. 503). Reframing the climate change debate by using the term "beyond reasonable doubt" may be a way to be forceful about the quality of the data and using an existing legal master frame. It also underscores that that doubting climate change now is simply unreasonable, and enough evidence has been proven to.

For the same reason, both scientists and journalists should use as much as possible the term "scientific fact" or "fact" when talking about man-made climate change. According to the National Center for Science Education (n.d.), a fact in science is *"an observation that has been repeatedly confirmed and for all practical purposes is accepted as "true." Truth in science, however, is never final and what is accepted as a fact today may be modified or even discarded tomorrow"* (par. 2). Therefore, "scientific fact" is the accurate term to use since climate science nearly unanimously agree that man-made climate change is happening – making it accepted as "true".

Proposed solutions:

1. Journalists should use the term "beyond reasonable doubt" to explain the certainty of climate science. Furthermore, they should reinforce that at least 97% of climate scientists agree that global warming/man-made climate change is happening.

2. Scientists should overcome their reticence and call climate change a "scientific fact" or "fact" when talking about man-made climate change. They also should be willing to point out that there is no more basis for denial of climate change than for denying that the earth is round (compare deniers to the Flat Earth Society), showing how ridiculous climate change denial actually is.

References

Bandura, A. (1977). Self-efficacy: Toward a unifying theory of behavioral change. *Psychological Review, 84*(2). doi:10.1037/0033-295X.84.2.191

Bandura, A. (1982). Self-efficacy mechanism in human agency. *American Psychologist, 37* (2): 122–147. doi:10.1037/0003-066X.37.2.122

Benford, R. D., & Snow, D. A. (2000). Framing processes and social movements: An overview and assessment. *Annual Review of Sociology, 26*, 611-639. doi: 10.1146/annurev.soc.26.1.611

Code of Ethics. (1996). Preamble. *Society of Professional Journalists.* Retrieved from https://www.spj.org/ethicscode.asp

Fessmann. J. (2016). The emerging field of public interest communications. In E. Oliveira, A. D. Melo & G. Goncalves (Eds.). *Strategic communication in non-profit organizations: Challenges and alternative approaches* (pp. 13-34). Wilmington: Vernon Press.

Fessmann, J., (2017). Conceptual foundations of public interest communications. *Journal of Public Interest Communications, 1*(1), 16-30. http://dx.doi.org/10.32473/jpic.v1.i1.p16

Fessmann. J. (2018). On communications war: Public interest communications and classical military strategy. *Journal of Public Interest Communications, 2*(1), 156-172. http://dx.doi.org/10.32473/jpic.v2.i1.p156

Festinger, L. (1957). *A theory of cognitive dissonance.* Evanston, Ill: Row, Peterson.

Foxall, G. R. (1990). *Routledge consumer research and policy series. Consumer psychology in behavioural perspective.* Florence, KY: Taylor & Frances/Routledge.

Gandy, O. H. (1982). *Beyond agenda setting: Information subsidies and public policy.* Norwood, NJ: Ablex Publishing Company.

Goffman, E. (1974). *Frame analysis: An easy on the organization of experience.* Cambridge, MA: Harvard University Press.

Howe, P. D., Mildenberger, M., Marlon, J.R., & Leiserowitz, A. (2015). Geographic variation in opinions on climate change at state and local scales in the USA. *Nature Climate Change, 5*(6), 596-603. doi:10.1038/nclimate2583

Hawken, P. (2017). *Drawdown: The most comprehensive plan ever proposed to reverse global warming.* New York, NY: Penguin Books

Kenner, R. & Robledo, M. [Producers], Kenner, R. [Director]. (2014). *Merchants of Doubt* [Motion Picture]. United States: Sony Pictures Classics

Kuhn, T. S. (2012). *The structure of scientific revolutions.* Chicago, IL: The University of Chicago Press.

Last Week Tonight with John Oliver (2014, May 11). Climate Change Debate [Video]. Retrieved from https://www.youtube.com/watch?v=cjuGCJJUGsg

McCright A.M., Dunlap, R.E. (2000). Challenging global warming as a social problem: an analysis of the conservative movement's counter-claims. *Social Problems, 47*(4), 499–522. DOI: 10.2307/3097132

MichaelEMann (2018, May 16). Latest #WallStreetJournal op-ed "The Sea Is Rising, but Not Because of Climate Change". Stay tuned for these great followup @WSJ op-eds: "Objects are falling, but Not Because of Gravity" "Continents are moving, but Not Because of Plate Tectonics" [Tweet]. Retrieved from: https://twitter.com/MichaelEMann/status/996794662487756800

National Center for Science Education (n.d.). Definitions of fact, theory, and law in scientific work. Retrieved from https://ncse.com/library-resource/definitions-fact-theory-law-scientific-work

Singer, F. (2018, May 15). The sea is rising, but not because of climate change. *The Wall Street Journal,* Opinion. Retrieved from https://www.wsj.com/articles/the-sea-is-rising-but-not-because-of-climate-change-1526423254?redirect=amp#click=https://t.co/GW7NHaZamT

Snow, D. A., & Benford, R. D. (1988). Ideology, frame resonance, and participant mobilization. *International Social Movement Research, 1*(1), 197-217.

Solutions Journalism Network (n.d.). Who we are. Retrieved from https://www.solutionsjournalism.org/who-we-are/mission

Tzu, S. (1910). *Sun Tzu and the art of war.* Lionel Giles (Trans.). (2000): Leicester, United Kingdom: Allandan Online Publishing.

Index

CPSIA information can be obtained
at www.ICGtesting.com
Printed in the USA
LVHW050047120419
613856LV00005B/23/P

9 781622 736300